To Pauline +
Caroline Hurr.
Feb 8ᵗ 2018.

A Modern-Day
Jonah

BRIAN BRADLEY

ACKNOWLEDGMENTS

I would like to begin by thanking my Lord and Saviour, Jesus Christ, for his constant and thoroughly undeserved goodness to me. I have experienced his grace and mercy in great abundance throughout my life, as the story that follows reveals.

I could not write acknowledgements without bearing testament to the absolute faith, love and generosity of my wonderful wife, Rosemary. She was everything I could have hoped for and so much more.

Our son Giles has been a delight to us both since the day he was born. I am so proud that he continues to follow our Lord wholeheartedly, and grateful for his careful attention to this book.

I also owe a great debt to my sister Caroline. She has been an incredible support to me and has dedicated a great deal of time to making sure this account of my life is accurate and readable.

This book would not have been possible without Joy Tibbs, who wrote and edited my memoir, based on a number of interviews and copies of reports I had submitted to my superiors over the years.

Thanks also to cover designer Lucy Thorne for her excellent work on the artwork for this book.

Finally, a great thanks to all those I have met along the way, who have inspired, challenged and encouraged me in my ministry and walk with God.

*To my darling Rosemary
and our much-loved son, Giles*

CONTENTS

FOREWORD

We sailed into Sri Lanka on the *Logos* in the early seventies, not realising all that God had in store for us. Meeting Brian and Rosemary Bradley birthed a friendship that would last the rest of our lives.

The success of our relationship boiled down to prayer and regular correspondence. We were reunited when they visited the *Logos II* in London in the nineties, and enjoyed another wonderful meeting at their home in Exmouth. I recently visited Brian for a special time of prayer and fellowship.

The following seven words come to mind as I think of Brian and Rosemary. These sentiments have been fortified as I have read through this book, which I hope you will read and share with others.

1. **Salvation.** The greatest event in Brian's life came about when he put his faith in the Lord Jesus (see chapter two). There were lots of bumps along the road both before and after that great event, which you will read about in this account.
2. **Bible.** Brian has always been a man of the Word. When he shared, the Word of God was his

the Word distributed, especially in Sri Lanka.

3. **Prayer.** Brian is a man of prayer. I think he has prayed for my wife and me, and for Operation Mobilisation (OM), for more than forty years. He has followed up on his prayers with action, often writing very encouraging letters.

4. **Generosity.** His willingness to go the extra mile for people is a legacy he can pass on to us through this book. He is a sacrificial giver, and we at OM benefited from that, as did many others.

5. **Love.** The most important aspect of our lives should always be love. As you read this book, I am sure that something of the revolution of love Brian knows and lives out will grip your heart.

6. **Vision.** Brian has always been able to mix local vision with global vision, and I guess that's one of the reasons he embraced OM, and particularly our ships. It's exciting to read here about his great ministry among seamen, who in many ways represent an unreached people.

7. **Perseverance.** Well into his senior years, and even as I write this, Brian's life is a loud message in itself. He is still doing what he can, despite some of the limitations of growing older. He will eventually finish the race, Rosemary having gone before him, and there will be a loud "Well done!" in heaven when he does.

George Verwer
Founder of Operation Mobilisation (OM)

INTRODUCTION

Facing me on the windowsill as I write is a small wooden plaque. Neatly burnt onto it are these words from Philippians 4:19 (KJV):

"But my God shall supply all your need according to His riches in glory by Christ Jesus."

This plaque was given to me in April 1978 by a Christian couple with whom my wife Rosemary and I were staying in Switzerland. Their lovely house was perched high up in the mountains above Château-d'Oex.

During our brief stay, we spoke one evening about some of our favourite Bible promises and I mentioned this one in particular. I was delighted when, just before we left, they presented me with this plaque, which they had made. I would like to explain why this promise means so much to me.

Beside me is a tiny pocket diary from 1959. In the small space below Thursday, 17th December, I had written:

"Received £2 anonymously by post – wonderful answer to this

evening's prayer!"

At this time, I was on vacation from the London College of Divinity, having completed my first year's training for the ministry. Like many students, I was broke, but had managed to get a job at the Post Office over the Christmas period.

While cycling home that evening, and just moments before I reached Le Bourg – a big house with a gun slit in the wall, which served as a reminder of German occupation, as the Nazis had commandeered the house during the war – I suddenly realised that I couldn't afford to buy my parents a present as I wouldn't be paid until after Christmas! I immediately prayed that God would forgive me for my careless stewardship, and meet my most urgent need by that day's post.

On reaching home, I saw some mail awaiting me and noticed, with a thrill, that one of the envelopes was registered! It contained two one-pound notes, but there was no accompanying letter.

Mystified, I upended and shook it, and out fell a tiny scrap of paper, which fluttered to the floor. It appeared blank, but on turning it over I saw written there "Phil. 4:19". I rushed to my Bible and looked up this reference. What an unforgettable answer to prayer!

The day before, a young lady named Joan had been walking down Smith Street when she suddenly stopped. She later confided to my younger sister Caroline that God had clearly told her at that moment that she was to send me some money straightaway by post.

Joan was standing opposite the Post Office, as it happened. She crossed the road, took out two pound notes and posted it off to me in a registered envelope, together with the Bible reference. I received that precious gift the next day, just moments after making the earnest request to my heavenly Father.

I can testify that, from the time before I met Rosemary, throughout our forty-seven years of marriage, and even now that she has gone to be with our heavenly Father, our faithful God has wonderfully met all our needs through our Saviour, Jesus Christ.

This book describes my journey of discovering the gospel, then trying to escape from God through my wilful disobedience to his clear call upon my life, before serving him in ministry along with my God-given wife. This lifelong voyage has taken me across the globe and exposed me to many miraculous experiences that are etched into my memory all these years on.

As you read my story, I pray that you will see that the indescribably wonderful life Jesus desires for each one of us will satisfy your deepest hopes and longings if you're prepared to trust and follow him.

1. THE ADVENTURE BEGINS

"For we are God's handiwork, created in Christ Jesus to do good works, which God prepared in advance for us to do."

Ephesians 2:10

My life began in Hong Kong back in 1932. My father was in the colonial service and served our government there, with periods of annual leave, for a total period of some ten years. When I was two, my parents, older sister Patty, younger brother Jeremy and I returned to Guernsey. Although I don't remember much about Hong Kong, I believe my great sense of adventure and love for travel stems back to those early days.

On our return, we lived with my grandparents in their Guernsey home, 'La Monnaie', which had lovely grounds. My father was posted to Uganda shortly afterwards and went on ahead to prepare for our arrival. Jeremy and I travelled out to Entebbe by boat and train with our mother to join him a few weeks later. For some reason or other, it wasn't considered safe or wise for young girls to travel to Africa at that time, so Patty remained in Guernsey with our grandparents.

A trip to Uganda

Our time in Uganda was memorable for all sorts of reasons, not least because I had acute appendicitis while I was out there. Healthcare standards were quite different back then, and I still have a very jagged scar to bear witness to the experience. I remember lying in hospital and my parents coming to visit me, laden with presents. Despite the pain, it was quite an exciting episode.

On another occasion, I remember a huge tree being cut down in the grounds of our Uganda home and finding it rather spell-binding. There were mango trees everywhere, and my love of mangoes has lasted right into my eighties.

We were in Uganda for a couple of years and I remember going on safari with my parents. Driving through the great open plains and seeing breath-taking nature up close was truly unforgettable. I don't think I realised then how fortunate we were to have these incredible experiences at such a tender age. Many of my peers never left British shores as youngsters, and some have remained close to home all their lives.

On one occasion, we travelled to Mount Elgon, and I remember looking up at it with awe. The countryside was like nothing I had ever seen before. We didn't climb the four-thousand-foot mountain, but a couple of decades later I attempted to climb Africa's tallest mountain, Mount Kilimanjaro.

The great escape

We returned to Guernsey when I was six, and more wonderful memories were made there. I remember playing a version of catch with Jeremy, which involved throwing a ball to each other over the roof of my grandparents' house.

I also had an air gun, which I'm ashamed to say I put to ill use. There was a lovely old stone archway outside the house, and I would sit about twenty yards from it and take pot-shots at sparrows as they played about on the ivy. I'm afraid I killed one or two, which fills me with horror now, as I'm so very fond of birds, but we took our excitement wherever we could in those days.

The Germans had been keeping an eye on the Channel Islands for some time and were planning an imminent invasion, so those of school age, myself included, were to leave the island for a safer destination in England. None of us had a clue where we would end up.

It was close to midnight when we gathered outside Elizabeth College back in 1940. The night was dark and cold, and there was a strong sense of fear in the air. You could almost taste it. Our headmaster addressed us in an attempt to calm our fears, but it wasn't fear that I felt; it was excitement. At the age of eight, I couldn't dwell on the dangers of war, either for myself or for those left behind. I looked upon the whole affair as a great opportunity for new experiences. This deep sense of adventure I was cultivating would be both a blessing and a curse in the years that followed.

We marched in pairs down the hill towards the harbour. The walk was about a mile long, and each step seemed to take us closer to the next chapter of our lives. We each wore gas masks around our necks, which clunked against our chests as we walked. Tucked into our buttonholes were labels confirming that we were evacuees. Clutched in my gloved hands was a packet of sandwiches for the journey.

It was only when I saw my maternal grandparents standing on the quayside with tears in their eyes that I felt a slight pang of guilt. There they were feeling sad and worried about our departure, while I was keenly awaiting the arrival of the mail boat that would take us to England and change our lives forever.

They waved us off as we sailed out of the harbour towards Weymouth, and we settled down for the choppy crossing. As it turned out, it was the last mail boat to leave the island before the Germans arrived on Guernsey's shores. How different my life might have been had we stayed on the island just a few days longer.

I didn't know it at the time, but those who stayed in Guernsey made life as difficult as possible for the Germans during the occupation. The locals changed street signs in a bid to cause maximum confusion, among other initiatives. I'm not sure the invading troops quite knew what they were letting themselves in for when they arrived on the island!

I never saw my grandfather again as he died during the war, but my grandmother lived into her eighties. Fortunately, my grandfather was not transported to a prison camp, as many of the men on the island were. As a member of the permanent jury (a 'jurate', as they were known under Normandy law), he was considered necessary to be part of the now-puppet government of the island. We received Red Cross messages from my grandparents while we were in England, so we had some contact, but we missed living with them despite the new adventures that were opening up for us.

Life as a refugee

When we arrived in Weymouth, we had to sleep on mattresses on the floor of a cold dormitory for a week or two. Did we mind? Not a bit of it! Next, we were moved up to a place near Buxton, as it was considered safer there than on the south coast. I was there for about a term, which was plenty of time to get up to some mischief.

Returning from a raid somewhere 'up north', the Germans disposed of their bombs almost on our doorstop in Great Hucklow. Like the band of merry hooligans we were, we considered this very exciting and made trophies of the pieces of shrapnel we found in the aftermath.

We walked everywhere 'in crocodiles' (pairs), and were pretty riotous most of the time. I feel sorry now for the staff who were looking after us! We spent much of our free time in what we called Sherwood Forest; an area that was believed to be part of the original Robin Hood territory. We would form gangs and throw stones at each other, which was mostly playful, although I vividly remember a young lad being carried away with blood pouring from his head on one occasion. Thankfully, he recovered and no real harm was done.

After this term up north, I was sent to Henley-on-Thames to join Jeremy in living with our 'aged aunts': Great-aunt Ginny and her long-term companion and housekeeper, Gabey, who was more like one of the family by this time. They were, in reality, only in their fifties, but as children we considered them to be very old. Ginny and Gabey were lovely women. Ginny was very much the decision-maker, while Gabey quietly loved and supported us. I'm so grateful for all they did. Gabey encouraged me to make a book of clippings about the war, which I still have today and is something of a relic, while Ginny made key decisions about my education, which had lasting implications.

We listened to the radio a good deal in those days, and when the national anthem was played, Ginny had us stand up to sing 'God Save the King'. We knew that she had lost her fiancé, whom she had adored, in World War One, but didn't understand how difficult she must have found life at this time, or what a great burden we must have been.

Whenever the air raid sirens went off, we trudged down into a deep cellar inside the house. After a while, we got used to them as they were so frequent. I suppose there must have been a little fear and anxiety in our hearts, but we were too young to fully understand how dangerous the situation was.

There were troop movements all over the place as Britain prepared for D-Day. Tanks regularly rumbled down New Street, where we lived. We sensed that the war would soon be over, and there was a real feeling of anticipation and excitement. I remember seeing British bombers flying overhead and the thrill of it all.

Jeremy and I often shinned up a small chestnut tree in our great aunts' garden at this time. We would walk along an old granite-and-flint wall, which was about ten feet high and fifty feet long, before climbing back down. It was a bit of adventure, but it always seemed quite safe.

One unforgettable day, we were walking along the wall and I said, "This is strange, Jeremy. The wall doesn't seem straight at all." Nevertheless, we managed to complete our usual walk and clamber back down without incident.

However, while we were having lunch, there was a tremendous roar, like an earthquake. We rushed out and the whole wall had collapsed as a result of the rumbling tanks! Huge great pieces of brick and flint had been thrown across the width of the garden. I don't honestly think Jeremy and I would have survived had we been on that wall just thirty minutes earlier!

Meeting the family

We hadn't seen our parents throughout the war, and I remember greeting them with a certain formality when I met them again at the age of fourteen. I held out my hand to greet them with a cordial handshake. I'm rather embarrassed now, as I was a little hard on them, but it felt as though we hardly knew them by this time.

My younger sister Caroline had been born in Uganda, so we met her for the first time at this point. At the age of four, she was perplexed and quite angry that these 'grown-ups' were making demands on *her* mummy and had a few tantrums about it. She was very sweet, though, and we soon became firm friends. We returned to Guernsey as a family, but my father soon received his next posting and sailed for Kuala Lumpur, Malaysia. My mother and Caroline remained in Guernsey but later joined my father for a period of six months. Caroline enjoyed the wildlife but has terrible memories of her time in school while she was there.

My life had felt like a series of adventures up to this point, and I knew there would be plenty more to come. What I didn't realise for many years was that there was only one cure for my constant desire for excitement, and that was a relationship with Jesus Christ. It took me far too long to realise that the very greatest adventure is doing God's will wholeheartedly!

2. ENCOUNTERING JESUS

"And we know that in all things God works for the good of those who love him, who have been called according to his purpose."
Romans 8:28

As a result of my Great-aunt Ginny's influence, it was decided that I would attend Lancing College from the age of thirteen to eighteen. She was very religious, and believed that the school's high church setting and excellent academic record would stand me in good stead.

A passion for sports

While I struggled academically due to undiagnosed dyslexia, my time at Lancing gave me the opportunity to become a serious athlete. I was absolutely mad about sports. I had always enjoyed being outdoors, particularly running, and Lancing College was the perfect place to hone my skills. It was all sports for me in those days. Work was very much a secondary consideration as far as I was concerned.

I was captain of boxing, cross-country running and athletics at Lancing, and people looked up to me for nothing more than being fast on the track or for holding my own in the ring. Sportsman though I am from the tips of my toes to the top of my head, I feel that people look up to sportsmen and women in a ridiculous way. I remember even back then feeling uncomfortable about having younger pupils run errands for me simply because I was good at sports, but that was just one of the strange public-school traditions I came up against.

I was taken down a peg or two when our sports master encouraged me to take on a boxer who was a boxing weight above me in a school match, which is an unreasonable ask at any level. Unsurprisingly, I didn't win that fight! However, I was awarded school colours for tennis and performed consistently well in running events, particularly cross-country.

I even played at Wimbledon on one occasion, albeit during the public schools' championships rather than in the official tournament. We played doubles on the outer courts against a couple from Eton. One of them was 'Lord so and so', and sadly we lost, but it was a great experience. I also sold ice creams during the official Wimbledon tournament one week. It was tricky handing over sweet treats when all I wanted to do was watch the action. I've always loved Wimbledon and still do.

Religious encounters
At this time, I thought I was a fairly good Christian because I attended a well-known Anglo-Catholic public school and we went to a short evening service on weekdays. On Sundays, we received sermons from six feet above contradiction, given by people with lots of letters after their names.

I remember two specific religious experiences I had as a youngster. The first was attending confession at Ginny's behest. I went along and was given a list of potential sins to remind me of all the bad things I may or may not have done. I didn't feel happy about it, as it didn't feel real at all. The priest sat behind a screen and listened to me as I confessed my sins. I thought it was absolute nonsense even at that age. I only went the once, but that was enough for me.

The second experience was that of my confirmation, which took place at our parish church in Henley-on-Thames at around the age of twelve. The only thing I can remember is that the naughty boy sitting behind me put a drawing pin down on my seat while we were standing, and I sat down on it! Ouch! I was confirmed long before I had any real understanding of the gospel or even heard of needing to be 'born again'. It was just pomp and ceremony to me, and it had no impact whatsoever on my heart or soul.

The Oxford experience

I left Lancing having passed my School Certificate but without getting my matriculation, which was the formal requirement to get into Oxford University. I received further tuition in Latin and maths back in Guernsey so that I could get into Oxford, to which my high-flying ancestors had paved a path.

My great-grandfather, George Granville Bradley, had been elected master of University College Oxford long before my time there and later became Dean of Westminster, so I had a lot to live up to! Incidentally, he also officiated at the Golden Jubilee service for Queen Victoria in 1887, presided at the coronation of Edward VII in 1901, and was altogether quite a character in himself.

I somehow got into Oxford, although I suspect my eminent ancestry had something to do with it. For some unknown reason, I had decided to study Modern History, which wasn't what I had expected it to be. I had to study the politics of Aristotle, and the French Revolution in French. We also had to study *Bede's History of England* in Latin. It seems crazy now. I was hopeless at Latin! All these decades later I still can't understand it.

I had never been to lectures before, and I found that I couldn't cope academically, although I was very much in my element from a sporting perspective. Sport was taken very seriously indeed at Oxford, and having run against well-known clubs at Lancing, I was honoured to be invited onto the cross-country team, the Tortoise Club as it was called then, by Chris Chataway, who was later knighted and became a member of parliament. He was the man who helped Roger Bannister break the four-minute mile.

It was a particularly good year for Oxford, because not only did the first team sweep the board, but I came first against Cambridge in the second team and we had the first four men home in that race. I was considered a pretty sure deal for the Oxford Blue, an award given for those competing at the highest level.

A real Christian

While I didn't know it at the time, God was to use my love of sport to speak into my life just before I turned twenty. One day on the running track, Julian Charley, a chap I didn't know from Adam, came jogging up to me, panting. We were preparing for a match against Cambridge, and as we attempted to catch our breath between laps, he said something that changed my life forever: "Brian, I want to tell you that my whole life has been completely transformed as a result of coming to know Jesus as my Lord and Saviour."

Despite my previous religious experiences, I had never heard anyone use language like this before and was absolutely intrigued. I knew instantly that this chap had the real thing. This was what I had unwittingly been searching for. I don't know if my mouth fell open, but it shook me rigid!

I went with Julian to a very evangelical church called St Ebbe's, and I heard the gospel as I had never heard it preached before. It was made very clear that I needed to respond, and that my life needed to change. I had thought I was a fairly decent Christian, but I finally realised how much I needed God. It suddenly occurred to me that one isn't born a Christian, and cannot become one by attending a church school.

One day, I knelt by my bedside and prayed. I said that I wanted to be a real Christian like Julian and asked the Lord to forgive me. I meant it from the very depths of my heart. I wanted to be an out-and-out Christian, and I knew that God had heard me. I was born again right there and then, and my life was changed forever, although I had a few 'Jonah moments' along the way.

Devastating exam failure
However, my time at Oxford was about to run out. I failed my prelims (preliminary examinations) and was allowed to retake them, probably riding on the coat-tails of my great-grandfather, but I failed with distinction the second time round. This hit me extremely hard. I felt as though I had let everyone down, not least because my predecessors had done so well.

I also narrowly missed out on getting my Oxford Blue when I was beaten into second place in a trial for the first team by a chap I normally would have beaten. Despite my exam failure, the Blue would have been a feather in my cap, and one that I felt I had earned. There was a great deal of kudos involved in that, and it surely would have softened the blow.

I felt completely bereft and blamed God. "Why had he allowed this to happen?" I asked myself over and over again.

I went to see the Dean of Oxford, and we agreed that even if I retook my exams I wouldn't pass them. However, having heard that I had been converted, he said something that was truly encouraging, although I didn't fully appreciate it at the time. He said: "Brian, don't worry about the future. Entrance into the kingdom of heaven is far more important than passing your preliminary exams."

I had failed my exams, but had gained a 'BA'. I was born again!

3. ON THE RUN

"Where can I go from your Spirit? Where can I flee from your presence? If I go up to the heavens, you are there; if I make my bed in the depths, you are there. If I rise on the wings of the dawn, if I settle on the far side of the sea, even there your hand will guide me, your right hand will hold me fast."

Psalm 139:7-10

Feeling utterly depressed at failing my exams, and with no clear path set out for me, I did something I would soon come to regret. Like a modern-day Jonah, naïve and young in my faith, I turned my back on God and decided to run away. The devil had a real go at me at this time, although I didn't recognise it as that. I wasn't swallowed by a whale, but I had many adventures and some truly difficult times in the five years that ensued.

Inspired by my father's overseas endeavours, I decided to join the colonial police in Tanganyika (now Tanzania). My father's younger brother had done very well in the colonial service and had been knighted Sir Kenneth Bradley. He was in charge of the Imperial Institute in London when it changed to the Commonwealth Institute. He also wrote a number of books, one of which was a must-read for anyone going into the colonial service. He was district commissioner in various places in Africa, including the Gold Coast, and his last stint was as chief secretary of the Falkland Islands. Once again, I had a lot to live up to!

A divine encounter

I had to travel to London for my interview, and during the train journey there I met a man who had a profound impact on my life, albeit in a delayed fashion.

While sitting in the dining saloon, a young clergyman named Eric James came and sat opposite me. He was a curate in London at the time. We got chatting and, knowing nothing of my exam failures, and to my great surprise, he leant across the table and said, "Brian, I think God has his hand upon you and wants you to train for the Church."

I thought, "Who is this stranger, speaking to me like this?" I had already hardened my heart and couldn't understand what business it was of his.

Anyway, he pressed on and I was very mystified by what he was saying. Before he got off the train, he told me he wanted to keep in touch and asked for my address. It was getting a bit too warm for my liking! Not sure which address to give, I rather cheekily gave him that of the police headquarters in Dar es Salaam, Tanganyika. I hadn't even been accepted by the police at this point!

He passed me a little card that I still have today, which said: "Do only what you can offer to God" on the front. On the back, he wrote, "For Brian from Eric, 03.05.1953". I thought I had done enough to keep him quiet and never expected to hear from him again.

I was subsequently accepted for my training and headed up to the training camp at Mill Meece near Stoke-on-Trent. While there, I did the ordinary basic traini any police bobby would have done at that time befor they went on the beat. Then I went down with the other colonial candidates to Hendon Police College, and remained there for about four months.

Among other things, we were taken into a morgue and shown the difference between the lungs of someone who had never smoked and the lungs of a heavy smoker. I remember this because it really put me off smoking! Avoiding the habit had always been common sense to me because I was so interested in athletics, but the memory stuck in my mind.

There followed a brief stint of two weeks in Southampton. I was attached there just to see what it would be like to operate from a police station in England. It was all new and exhilarating, so I went out to East Africa full of excitement towards the end of December 1953.

Life in Tanganyika
On reaching Dar es Salaam, we lived at the police mess with the other cadet superintendents. This sounds terribly grand, but in those days all the white cadets were officers. I found myself living with a bunch of cadets who were just out for a jolly good time. Being a long way from home, they got up to all sorts of mischief.

I still considered myself a Christian, albeit a disobedient one, and I knew they were carrying on a rather lively lifestyle. They didn't have any sort of beliefs and were quite immoral, jumping in and out of bed with women all over the place. I'm ashamed to say I wasn't living as I should have been, but, in his great mercy, God kept me from going completely overboard.

I remember my conscience overtaking me in the following weeks, and the time came when I realised I wasn't going to be happy in the Tanganyikan police. I had begun to realise that my encounter with God at Oxford, and my meeting with Eric on the train, had been no accident. I felt compelled to go and see the police commissioner.

Full of nerves, I went in and explained that God had placed a calling on my life, and that this wasn't it. I knew that I needed to return to England to discover exactly what he wanted me to do. That must have come as quite a shock to the commissioner! However, he pointed out that if I left without fulfilling my two-and-a-half-year contract, I would have to refund several hundred pounds to the government for my training and pay for my travel there and back. I didn't have the means to do that, so there was nothing for it but to stay and fulfil my contract.

This was an important lesson and a testing time. I felt trapped and it was difficult sticking it out when I knew that it wasn't God's plan for my life. I had plenty of adventures and excitement at this time, but no happiness. I had come to realise that you can't run away from God.

There were problems in Tanganyika at this time because of the Mau Mau uprising in neighbouring Kenya, so it was quite a dangerous posting. There were many people who wanted the British out, which is understandable in a colonial territory, although most of the people we met were quite friendly and appreciated the many good things the Brits had done there.

During a spell up in Mwansa, a town on Lake Victoria near the southern border, I was detailed by my boss to take a company of 'askaris' (local policemen) to a place near the Kenyan border because the district commissioner needed help. I was in charge of some forty to fifty men, and we travelled up on this assignment in a few of our available trucks.

I was told to clear away some people who were thought to be involved with the Mau Mau. I was told to surround the area as no one was supposed to be living there because of the danger of tsetse fly, which was a major carrier of malaria. It was my job to ensure that the order, which stipulated that no one should be living there, was enforced.

It was the first time I had ever pulled out my revolver in anticipation. We weren't sure whether the men living there were just poachers or were really up to no good. Thankfully, there was nobody in the huts when we surrounded it, as I had been ordered to clear everyone out and burn the huts down.

We found one or two guns there, but it was quite clear that they were simply poachers rather than terrorists. Had we encountered people there that day we would have had to capture or even kill them, depending on how they responded, so I was glad the Lord spared me such a confrontation.

Once or twice I got a message through saying there had been a serious accident up country. The dirt-track 'roads' were terrible, and the locals had a habit of climbing on top of the lorries and trains, which was very dangerous. On these occasions, I had to go and investigate what had happened and write a report.

I was called out one time because somebody had spotted a body in a ditch, so I had to go up there, fish the body out and bring it back to headquarters. It was the first time I had ever taken the fingerprints of a dead man. I can assure you, it wasn't easy!

I loved spear fishing when I was in Dar es Salaam. In those days, it was considered a good sport. I never actually used diving gear, but I snorkelled, which was quite fun. One of my friends and I caught rather a big fish once, which we took back to the police mess and ate for dinner.

At another time, there was a report of rabies in the area and I was asked to go out and shoot any dogs I saw. It was an unpleasant but necessary task, and I counted thirteen in total.

A mountain to climb

At one point, I was posted to a place called Moshi up near Arusha; a very beautiful part of the world. I was doing a refresher course at the police training centre out there. For a time, I was working for the traffic police. This still makes me laugh as my late wife Rosemary and I often joked about my hopeless sense of direction. I hope I didn't lead too many people astray when they asked for directions! I had a police motorbike for a while, which helped me get around and I enjoyed this form of travel.

While I was in Moshi, a fellow cadet told me he was planning to climb Mount Kilimanjaro. The guide books say that it takes at least five days, but I had only managed to secure two-and-a-half days off. My friend had trained hard for a year or two in preparation, while I had done no training at all, arrogantly believing that I could do without it as I was pretty fit. I learnt my lesson the hard way.

We dispensed of the usual guides and porters, deciding to carry all our own things. The ascent began well, and we managed to get to sixteen thousand feet before I started to suffer extreme altitude sickness, including severe headaches. I'm pleased to say that we made it above the snow level. Some of the askaris with us had never touched snow before and were very excited. I can still picture them playing with it and throwing it up in the air.

My friend went on further and reached the summit, while I collapsed in a little hut, sick as a dog! Looking back, I wish I had been more sensible, but one learns from one's mistakes. The journey back to camp almost made up for the disappointment, as we travelled through the forest and saw some incredible sights. We even heard the trumpeting sounds of a herd of elephants at one point.

I was later posted to Kigoma, right over on the western border of Tanganyika, and south of Burundi. That was a wonderful trip. It was five miles from Ujiji, where Stanley famously met David Livingstone, giving rise to the phrase, "Dr Livingstone, I presume?" I visited the spot where the encounter took place and bought a stamp at the little post office as a keepsake.

While I was there, a letter arrived for me. It had been redirected from Dar es Salaam several times, but it had eventually caught up with me. I wondered who it might be from.

The letter began: "Dear Brian Bradley, we met on a train just over two years ago…" I certainly hadn't expected that!

It was from Eric James, who, remembering our meeting on the train, had been praying for me. He was chaplain of Trinity College Cambridge by this time. We exchanged one or two letters, and he invited me to come and see him when my time in Tanganyika ended. I wrote back and said that I was leaving the police, but wasn't sure what the future held for me.

A spell in Canada

Still practising the disobedience of Jonah, I returned to England in 1956, but I was still running away from God. I wasn't ready to go to the 'Nineveh' he had prepared for me and went to the equivalent of Jonah's 'Tarshish' instead.

I regret to say that I didn't go to see Eric. Instead, I took a job at my brother-in-law's prep school in Sussex for a term. One of the teachers was off sick, so I stood in for him, teaching Latin of all things. I had failed Latin at Lancing, but as it was only a junior form I just about managed it.

I was on the run again and for some reason I had set my sights on British Columbia, Canada. I was interviewed by *The Guernsey Press* about my trip before I went out there in March 1957. I spent a year in Vancouver, not knowing anyone there apart from some distant cousins, with whom I spent very little time. I did various jobs but struggled to find anything meaningful to do at a time when unemployment in Canada was high.

I worked at a petrol station for a week or so, and enjoyed driving one or two Cadillacs around the courtyard! I also did quite a lot of manual work, such as sweeping warehouses, to keep myself alive.

I remember working as a salesman at a large department store over the Christmas period. I was unpacking some toys to set out one day and found that they were enveloped in huge sheets of uncut paper. As I unfolded them, I realised they were parts of the New Testament, including chunks taken from John's Gospel. That really made me sit up and think! God was still speaking into my life, despite my disobedience.

I worked on a building site at one time and was asked to do a highly dangerous job on the shell of a building that was eight stories high. My boss stacked several bags of cement onto one of the hoists and my job was to unload them onto the top of the building. I had never had much of a head for heights, and there was quite a high wind that day.

I had one foot on top of the building and the other on the side of the hoist, spread over a large gap. It was only then that I thought, 'Gosh, I'm worth more than a bag of cement!' So I beetled down to my boss and informed him that I needed help. I wasn't going to risk my life to do this job. I probably only worked there for ten days, but it was enough for me and for my boss. I subsequently worked on an assembly line at a chainsaw factory for about two months, which was much safer comparatively!

The runaway on the runway
Regrettably, and shamefully, I still had no clear goal in front of me, but as I was walking down Barrard Street, one of Vancouver's best-known shopping areas, I spotted the recruiting office for the Royal Canadian Air Force just opposite me. I thought this might offer me a truly exciting and adventurous career. I popped in and was given a preliminary IQ test, which I managed to pass, and continued to do odd jobs while they were considering my application to become a pilot.

In due course, I underwent and passed a rigorous medical examination as well as an equally searching interview. So far so good! A month or two later, I was sent to Toronto in eastern Canada to undergo a vital two-week selection course.

Early on, each of us in turn was enclosed in a simulator representing the cockpit of a jet fighter plane. I staggered out like a drunk man. I didn't know my head from my heels, or whether I was coming or going, but I think the powers that be knew where I was going, and it wasn't into the Canadian Air Force!

I think they realised I would have been a very expensive liability; that I would probably kill myself and destroy one of their highly sophisticated, multi-million-dollar machines in the process. I was disappointed to have failed, but I knew deep down that I was still running away and that the air force wasn't really for me.

A change of heart

I found myself – with a few other failed candidates – crossing Canada again by train over the vast Canadian Prairies with only a dollar or two to my name. It was then that I finally came to my senses. I thought of Julian Charley and remembered the peace and joy I had felt the day that I had accepted Jesus Christ as my Lord and Saviour.

I remember praying, "Lord, I'm completely off track. Please forgive me for my continued disobedience in trying to run away from you these past few years. Please show me your will for me now."

Within half an hour, a delightful elderly lady had come and sat down opposite me. She introduced herself as Annie Ferguson and asked me a bit about my life. It turned out she had been a secretary at McGill University, and was eager to talk about her conversion, which had taken place at the university some years earlier. I immediately sat up and gave her my full attention.

Annie got off the train at a place called Banff in the Rockies, and I never saw her again, but she had told me that there was a church in Vancouver that she thought would be a real blessing to me. It was called the Alliance Tabernacle.

My mind immediately raced back to Henley-on-Thames and I remember thinking, "What would my dear Great-aunt Ginny think? What strange-sounding cult is this?" I had no idea what the church would be like, but I believed Annie's words were a direct answer to my prayer.

This time, I responded to God's leading and headed to the church one Sunday morning. I very nearly walked out, because it was what you might call a 'happy-clappy' place. The chap that got up to preach wasn't wearing a cassock or even a dog collar. He was wearing a bright red tie! Apart from my time at St Ebbe's, I had been accustomed to a high church background and wasn't used to such a casual approach. I just about stopped myself walking out, and when I heard the man preach I felt captivated once again. I realised this was what I had been missing out on all this time, and gave him my full attention.

I noted during the service that a preacher named J Sidlow Baxter was coming very soon to the Alliance Tabernacle on a tour of Canada from Scotland, so I returned to the church to hear him preach. He was there for a week or so and I went to each service, even though I had quite a journey to get there. That was a real turning point for me. I was finally ready to live all-in for God, as I had promised in my room in Oxford five years earlier.

Around this time, I met Bob Birch, the pastor of a church in the east end of Vancouver called the Reformed Episcopal Church. Again, I didn't know what this meant, but I went along anyway. I heard Bob preach and thought his message was absolutely super, so I kept attending the church. Everything he said was bang on!

I was staying in digs at the time, and Bob asked me if I would like to become a paying guest at the rectory. I was delighted and spent several months living with him and his wife Dorothy. I got to know Dorothy better than Bob as he was rather like an Old Testament prophet. Bob had been very ill and God had intervened in a dramatic way, so he was totally fired up for the Lord. He used to disappear downstairs at about two thirty in the morning to begin his devotions! He was a truly godly man.

The household used to take advantage of his absent-mindedness for a bit of fun. They would see how many times they could get him to say grace before a meal by repeatedly pausing and bowing their heads!

I was helping out in the Sunday school and reading my Bible again regularly for the first time in a long while, and it felt as though I was in some way fulfilling God's calling on my life. I had come to understand the strange Christian paradox that true freedom can only be experienced by those who learn to subject themselves to the claims of Jesus Christ, through the grace of the Holy Spirit. The Lord showed me the meaning and value of true discipleship at this time.

Back to Blighty

The day came when I felt God telling me quite clearly to return to England. I was beginning to feel that I would go anywhere he wanted me to, so I started to make preparations. I didn't know how I was going to get back, but I heard there was a chap in the army whose leave was about to run out.

This soldier had to get back to Toronto within a couple of days or he would be court-martialled! He had recruited a fellow driver, but was looking for a third person to take spells behind the wheel. The three of us drove day and night, covering two thousand eight hundred miles in just two-and-a-half days.

I woke up on the backseat at one point and realised we had stopped. One of the drivers had been speeding and we had to pay a fine! Apart from that, the journey progressed smoothly. I secured my passage on a small cargo boat from Halifax to England in April 1958. I was ready for my Nineveh experience and determined in my heart that I would never run away from God again.

Materially speaking, my Canadian venture proved unsuccessful, but spiritually I found lasting riches I had not sought. Even in our disobedience, God is faithful, and he turned everything to good for me. Having said that, I realised that I could have saved myself a lot of heartache if I had followed his guidance from day one!

4. BACK ON TRACK

"I will repay you for the years the locusts have eaten"
Joel 2:25

Living back in Guernsey, I earned a bit of money working at Wetherall, Drake and Co, the successful tomato-growing company my grandfather had set up. I planted seedlings and looked after the plants. That was quite a useful experience and provided the perfect analogy for my later life as a minister with numerous fledgling Christians under my care!

After my experience at Oxford, I had vowed never to open another study book, but I sensed more strongly than ever that God was calling me into the ministry at this time.

God's gracious provision

I managed to successfully apply for some funding from the Church Pastoral Aid Society (CPAS) to get me into college, and was offered a place at the London College of Divinity (LCD), which later became St John's, Nottingham. I had to take preliminary exams to get in, and the vicar, Revd Geary Stevens of St Stephen's

Church, Guernsey, was of tremendous help to me in this respect. It was a miracle that I got in, and I was so grateful to God for opening a door for me. Revd Stevens was a real man of God: a great preacher and a much-loved pastor. He was also a great help to me prior to my ordination.

All sorts of miracles occurred while I was at college. During my first term, the college secretary approached me and brought up the fact that I hadn't paid my fees. I knew that I didn't have the money, and that I was fully reliant on God's provision. I felt anxious and rather embarrassed not to be able to pay my way.

I sent up a desperate prayer: "Lord! You know that I haven't paid my fees yet and I haven't got enough money. Please, please send me some from somewhere."

Once again, a mysterious meeting on a train played an important part in my life at this point. I had met an elderly lady on a short journey a couple of weeks earlier and we had got chatting. She was on her way up to London to hear John Stott speak, and I had briefly prayed for her. I had told her that I was training for the ministry, but made no mention of fees or any money problems.

I was earnestly praying about the situation but couldn't see where an answer might come from. Out of the blue, and within two days of being asked for the funds, this lady sent me a cheque for a hundred pounds! It was quite astonishing to receive a financial gift at all, not to mention such a vast amount of money, as it was at the time. Talk about an answer to prayer!

I was beginning to learn just how faithful God was, and wished I had put my trust in him much sooner. This was just one of the many occasions when God wonderfully intervened on my behalf, and I am eternally grateful for his ongoing provision.

During the college holidays, God answered my prayers for money once again. I didn't have enough to buy Christmas presents for my parents, and desperately sought the Lord as I wanted to give them something, even if it was only a small gift. Unbeknown to me, as I was praying, he was moving on the heart of a dear woman to send me two pound notes when I really needed it. (See the Introduction for the full story.)

God knows our needs even before we ask, but he still likes us to ask!

Ups and downs

I lived on campus while I was at the London College of Divinity in Northwood and, in stark contrast to my time at the police mess in Tanganyika, where moral standards had been lax, I was surrounded by other Christians. I attended the college at the same time as George Carey, who later became Archbishop of Canterbury, and we both played for the college football team. He came from a difficult background but was a dear man.

Unfortunately, I struggled academically as I had at Oxford six years earlier, and I hadn't done any real studying since then. My peers went straight up into the second year, while I had to repeat my first year. This meant that it would take me four years to complete the three-year course.

One of the most vivid memories I have of theological college was a trip to Hyde Park Corner to present our testimonies, an experience that awaited every student during his final year at LCD. It was part of what we called our Church Army Weekend. Each student had three minutes on the soapbox, and it was a daunting challenge for each of us. I got up to speak and felt Satan on one shoulder, whispering lies into my ear. He never takes a holiday! He kept telling me that I was repeating myself and that I had made a complete mess of my testimony, but somehow I managed to get to the end of it before stepping down.

Feeling rather subdued, I was delighted when a man came up to me and said: "I was so interested in what you said. Can I see you to talk about it more?"

I told him that we students had to walk back to the Church Army headquarters straightaway behind their musical band, so we swapped addresses and kept in touch. Over a period of two to three months, we wrote to each other, and I was able to share more of the gospel with him.

Shortly before Easter, I received a letter from him, which said: "Brian, I want you to know that, in view of all you have told me, I have asked Jesus Christ into my heart as my Lord and Saviour."

I was so thrilled that God had been able to use my stammerings to bring someone into the kingdom. His strength is made perfect in our weakness, and even when we feel as though we may have said something foolish, God honours it. This was one of many occasions when the Lord used my testimony to speak to someone, and it still brings me true excitement to think of these 'chance' meetings. I have always loved sharing my testimony, and still do.

God has given me a certain easiness with people, and I thank him for that. From the world's point of view, I'm at the bottom of the heap academically – particularly compared with my ancestors – but God has a habit of using people like fishermen, tax collectors and failed Oxford students! In God's economy, I can rejoice in the fact that he uses the foolish things to confound the wise.

Caroline's conversion

It was around this time that the Lord used me to bring Caroline to a knowledge of Jesus as her Lord and Saviour. I was on vacation from theological college and had returned to Guernsey to stay with my family. She was eighteen at the time.

I remember sharing my testimony with my parents, my grandmother and Caroline over lunch one day, and telling them how my life had been wonderfully changed as a result of my conversion.

Our parents never talked about religion because, when they met, Mum was a devout Christian, while Dad had been brought up as a Christian Scientist and thrown it all out in disgust. Having argued extensively about religion while they were engaged, they had made a pact never to discuss the subject again.

After giving my testimony, there was a deadly silence, although I could see that Caroline was listening carefully. It was a very uncomfortable and embarrassing moment, and of course Satan was sitting on my shoulder once again telling me what a mess I had made of it.

Caroline disappeared to her bedroom, where she struggled with her conscience all afternoon. Eventually, she descended the stairs, hovering momentarily in the hall. Should she turn into the drawing room, where she could hear that the television was on, or into the dining room, where she guessed I was doing my studies?

She was propelled towards the dining room and opened the door to say, "Brian, I just want you to know that all I have ever wanted was to be a true Christian. I felt so sorry for you at lunchtime. It was so difficult for you, but I was very impressed by what you said."

God had been working in her life in all sorts of ways, but she certainly wasn't a born-again Christian at this time. Caroline had known Jesus as a distant figure whom she admired tremendously for dying for her sins. Our mother had always encouraged Caroline to read her Bible and attend church, as she did herself.

Our parents were not tactile, but our mother shared intimate times of prayer with Caroline at the end of each day. Mum would sit on the bed, while Caroline would kneel up with her arms crossed over our mother's shoulders. As she prayed, Caroline felt close to God because she felt close to her mother. She had earnestly sought God over the years, but there was still something missing.

"I would love to know Jesus as you do," she told me. We had a further discussion and I said, "If you like, I can pray for you and you can ask Jesus into your life."

I asked Caroline to kneel and surrender her will to God, and that was what really hit home for her. She followed my instruction and gave her heart to Jesus. The next day, Caroline read the story of Nicodemus in John 3 and remarked that the Bible had completely come alive for her.

She soon joined the only evangelical church in Guernsey at the time and a young woman there named Joan (as mentioned in the Introduction) took Caroline under her wing to disciple and encourage her. This was such a wonderful answer to my prayers, especially as I had felt so horribly embarrassed over lunch. It was a marvellous experience and reminded me of God's great faithfulness.

Not long after she had this life-changing experience, she took shorthand and typing lessons back in Guernsey. She was looking for a job, and I had an idea that I thought might just work out for her. During my time at LCD I had boarded with a man named Branse Burbridge.

He was a wonderful Christian who had started the war as a pacifist and, upon seeing his friends die in the effort, joined the air force and was later decorated for shooting down many enemy planes.

By this point, he was working for Scripture Union. At my request, he offered Caroline a job, which sent her into a panic as she hadn't long been born again. When she wrote to Branse explaining her concerns, he sent her a telegram telling her not to worry and to just come, so she moved to London. This was yet another wonderful answer to prayer.

Caroline and I prayed a great deal for my parents from this point on. Being closer to them, she was able to help them in their latter years. Most notably, she took my parents to a guest service one Sunday at All Souls Langham Place, the church she was attending in London, where Rev John Stott was the minister.

The preacher that day was none other than the Rev Julian Charley! As he had done for me on the running track, he presented the gospel message clearly, and when the invitation was given to walk to the front and kneel to receive Jesus as Saviour, my father responded, much to Caroline's joy.

He later told her that he had been reading the daily Bible passages from a Scripture Union diary she had bought him the following Christmas. Another time he showed her the wooden cross that he secretly wore around his neck and said, "I feel Jesus' presence with me every day."

Decades later, my dad was told he had cancer of the oesophagus, and before he died in 1991 I went over and said a prayer for him. By that time, I had absolute peace that he had become a Christian. I had the privilege of speaking at his funeral, with the full assurance that he was already in heaven.

My mother survived him for eleven years, and she also made a further commitment to God. She recognised that Caroline had a closer relationship with God than she did and longed to have the same experience. Caroline was able to pray with her several times.

Mum had dementia in her latter years, but before she died she kept a little Christian book I had given her called *The Reason Why* by her bed. I was so thrilled to see it there. Again, I felt sure that my mum had accepted Jesus as her Lord and Saviour, and I look forward to seeing them both when I reach heaven.

One of the fondest memories I have of my mother comes from the time of the Queen's coronation. She wanted to be there and persuaded us to camp out with the thousands of others who were desperate to catch a glimpse of our new monarch. We camped out on The Mall for thirty-six hours, which was very game of my mother, who wasn't in her first flush of youth! It was very wet, but I remember it being such a joyful occasion, and it was great to share it with my family as we had so few memories of traditional family life from childhood.

More exam failure

The final year of Bible college eventually came around, and I found myself in one of the deepest, darkest pits I had ever been in. My worst nightmare was realised when I failed my final exams, having already repeated the first year. I just couldn't believe it.

"Why would God have called me to ministry knowing that I couldn't pass the exams?" I wondered. "Am I just wasting my time?"

My friends and teachers recognised that I had an unusual calling on my life, but it was such a terrible moment and I don't think anyone knew what to say to me. I received some wonderful letters from people who had been at college with me, saying that they had been praying for me, but nothing quite consoled me as my future looked so truly bleak. I felt as though failure was following me around and that I would never succeed at anything. If you're feeling that way reading this, be encouraged. God has a purpose and a plan for your life!

I went to see the principal and he was scratching his head about what could be done. He knew that I wouldn't be able to pass even if I retook it, but was convinced that I had a future in the Church. He offered me a four-month placement writing essays for the Bishop of London at Ashburnham Place, and somehow this enabled me to scrape through my training.

I was finally ordained at St Paul's Cathedral in 1961. My parents did not attend, owing to the fact that they were visiting my brother Jeremy in New Zealand at the time. This was a great disappointment for me, as for the first time in my life I felt I had done something they could be proud of, although it was entirely down to God and his unending grace that I eventually got through it. It was a great comfort to me that Caroline was able to attend.

Newly ordained, I was ready to begin a life of ministry, but I still had no concept of the incredible adventures God had in store for me!

5. THE PERFECT FAMILY

"He who finds a wife finds what is good and receives favour from the Lord."

Proverbs 18:22

My first curacy was at St Stephen's, East Twickenham, which became a really thriving church, and still is to this day.

The first Sunday I was there, the vicar announced my arrival and encouraged members of the congregation to invite the new curate over for lunch so they could get to know me.

Falling in love

I duly received an invitation from a lady named Rosemary, who put on a lovely lunch. She was secretary to my first vicar at St Stephen's and worked in the same capacity at a prep school. She had also been leading the church's Pathfinders youth group for several years. I discovered that her first husband, who had been in the merchant navy, had died of cancer at a young age.

Before that, he had often been away with his work, which was difficult for Rosemary as the couple had two daughters, Lin and Jane. She had brought the girls up singlehandedly and on a shoestring since his passing, to her great credit.

She had been through a really tough time, but I could tell that she had a deep faith in God and that she was a truly special lady. I also soon realised, with some astonishment and joy, that she seemed to be interested in me!

In her diary that Christmas, entirely unbeknown to me, she wrote:

> *I spied coming into the hall a handsome young man…! I was introduced to him as Brian Bradley, the new curate! Within a few days, Norman asked me if I would like to give a meal to Brian, as he would be living in 'digs'…I agreed. The Lord certainly had His hand in that decision! Brian and I got to know each other through that lunch…*

> *I was completely smitten, though Brian was eight years younger than me, and there were a lot of unmarried females in the congregation who thought him attractive too!*

I was fascinated to learn that Rosemary had been born in Muzaffarpur, India, where her father was a sugar planter. Although she had moved to England with her mother at the age of five, she shared my heart for travel and was open to new experiences, which came in very handy later on. Rosemary had attended boarding school in Bexhill and later in London.

She loved playing tennis, as I did, and was also a great piano player, which was again very useful during our time in ministry. I later learnt that she had survived a brush with death during the war when a bomb exploded in her next-door neighbour's garden! It seemed we had a fair bit in common.

At the age of seventeen, Rosemary started sorting notes at the Bank of England, and was given a half-day holiday if a counterfeit was detected! In November 1942, she joined the Wrens. She trained in Brighton, and had she not been struck down with a bout of the measles, the chances are I would never have met her. It turned out that her contemporaries had been moved to the East Coast and several were killed by a bomb there.

Once she was back on her feet, Rosemary spent time in Newhaven servicing torpedoes and depth charges. On one occasion, she dropped a detonator down a ladder, and it landed at the feet of an officer, who wasn't best pleased! Fortunately, it didn't explode.

Rosemary had given her heart to the Lord in Orpington. Although the vicar wasn't a powerful preacher, he was a sound Christian and had a profound impact on her through his faithful teaching. Although I never had a chance to meet and thank him personally, I was so grateful to him for bringing Rosemary to Jesus. Her faith shone out of her, and was a great encouragement to me and everyone else she encountered.

I never met Rosemary's mother, who had died at a young age, but I met her father, a dear man who had once been in the Indian army. Rosemary also had a brother, David, who was great company. He was an architect and had been a pilot during the war. We spent quite a bit of time with David and his wife Joy during our courtship. Sadly, her other brother, Reggie, had been killed in a flying accident while serving with the Fleet Air Arm in 1944.

It wasn't long before I had fallen head over heels in love, and I knew the feeling was mutual. We got to know each other better, and although Rosemary was a widow with two children, and despite the fact that she was eight years my senior – certainly not what I had anticipated in a potential wife – I knew that I wanted to spend the rest of my life with her.

I am so deeply thankful that the Lord showed me in all sorts of ways whom he wanted me to marry. He always knows best!

Tying the knot

I proposed to Rosemary in Isabella Gardens, a lovely flower-filled piece of land not far from Richmond. It was a beautiful spot, and I chose it because we both loved horticulture and natural wildlife so dearly. Rosemary was very interested in flowers and I was very interested in birds. I presented her with a ring, which was given and received with much joy! We were both very excited about our future life together and couldn't wait to get started.

I remember looking across and locking eyes with her one Sunday in our church hall. No words were necessary as we silently communicated our deep love for one another. It was so memorable that we never forgot it. That one brief moment meant so much to us in all the happy years of marriage that were to follow.

We were married at St Stephen's in 1964, and it was a very special occasion. So many people we had known and loved over the years were there, which was a great blessing. An article in one of the local papers went as far as to describe it as the wedding of the year!

Lin was sixteen and Jane was thirteen when I married Rosemary. We had some tricky times with the two girls while they were teenagers, and it was a steep learning curve for me, but they were loveable girls, which bears great testament to Rosemary's incredible parenting skills.

To our delight, both girls married fine Christian men and now have amazing children of their own. Lin and Jane inherited their mother's love for beautiful gardens and classical music, as well as her ability to make friends very easily.

Rosemary knew I was planning to head overseas at some point, and fortunately she shared my travel bug. During all the adventures that followed our wedding, Rosemary was an absolutely fantastic support and travel companion.

A baby boy

The time came for me to leave my first curacy at St Stephen's, where we had made such great friends and experienced God's blessing on both our marriage and ministry. We knew that fresh adventures lay ahead wherever he was to take us, and the next step on the journey was a second curacy in Herne Bay, Kent, where I served for around four-and-a-half years.

Without a doubt, the best thing that happened while we were in Herne Bay was the birth of our precious son, Giles, in July 1965. He was born in Whitstable, not far from our adopted home. I would love to have been present at the birth, but things were very different back then and husbands were kept well away from the delivery suite. Nevertheless, we were both ecstatic to welcome our son into the world, and I couldn't have been prouder of my lovely wife. It was a very exciting time for our family, and Lin and Jane were thrilled to have a baby brother.

We would have loved to have more children, but sadly Rosemary suffered a miscarriage after this. We were both deeply saddened not to be able to give Giles a brother or sister, but the traumatic experience hit my dear wife particularly hard. I did what I could to support her, but it was a very difficult time. I thank God for his great comfort during that dark period and for giving us such a delightful son, who has been a constant source of joy to us.

Moving on

From Herne Bay, we moved to Wilton, near Middlesbrough, as a first step towards securing an overseas posting. I joined The Missions to Seamen and learnt the ropes from a man who had previously been in the RAF. I helped out at the church where he was in charge, and we all enjoyed the change of scenery.

The Missions to Seamen had grown from the work of John Ashley among seamen in the Bristol Channel during the nineteenth century. John, a young clergyman, was on holiday with his young son Johnnie when they saw the sun reflecting from a window on a nearby island. He wondered how the people living there were able to go to church, and the answer was that they couldn't and didn't.

He visited the islands regularly until the time came for him to leave Clevedon, but before he left he asked the islanders about the large fleet lying at anchor in the Penarth Roads, waiting for a favourable wind. He discovered that no one visited the ships' crews while they were in port, and went to see this particular ship's company. He decided to abandon the post he had been about to take up and devote himself to ministering to seamen instead. He had a cutter built and named her Eirene, which means 'peace', and added a chapel below decks. The services he held on deck were always well-attended.

Inspired by his work, other men opted to build on the foundations John had laid and the Bristol Channel Missions was established. By 1856, The Missions to

Seamen was born. The first secretary was WHG Kingston, a famous writer of sea stories. It was his wife and sister-in-law who made the first Flying Angel flag, which in time became a well-known symbol across the globe.

By the time I joined the mission, its work was being carried out in two hundred and fifty ports, ninety of them with full-time staff. These employees worked from Flying Angel Clubs, which provided recreational facilities where seafarers could relax away from their ships and any exploitative shore people. Activities at the centres ranged from dances to football matches and meals, with swimming pools proving a major attraction in ports with hotter climates.

The year before I joined, more than a million chaplain visits were recorded, reaching out to around eighty thousand ships in total. Chaplains were always welcome on board the ships and a great deal of counselling often took place, as stress is a major factor in seafaring life.

Chaplains were also able to pray with and host services for crew members who were open to hearing the gospel and to encourage any Christians among them with one-on-one prayer and fellowship. We were also tasked with visiting unfortunate seamen who had ended up in hospital or prison, which was an important ministry in its own right.

A maritime ministry

My colleague regularly visited ships on the Teesside docks, where the huge chemical plants were based, and I followed suit. It wasn't long before I started visiting some of the ships and driving a bus carrying seamen between their vessels and Flying Angel House, the mission's local base.

It was a nice, quiet place away from the docks, where the ships' crews could get some much-needed rest and relaxation. They had the opportunity to play table tennis or snooker at the mission, and sometimes football on a nearby pitch. We held social evenings at the base and screened several Chinese and Indian films for our guests from those countries, which gave them a little taste of home away from home.

We were also invited on deck by several of the ships, including the *MV River Ethiope*. Having accommodated the chief officer's two daughters at the vicarage for a couple of nights, we enjoyed a lovely lunch on board.

Another time, the Indonesian captain of the *Johannes Latuharhary* invited us on board for a candlelit banquet, which was a great occasion. Unfortunately, the ship's chief steward, Ibrahim Schram, contracted peritonitis before the ship sailed and was taken into hospital. We were able to put his wife up at Flying Angel House while he recovered. The Schrams were Christians and Mrs Schram joined us for Sunday worship during Mr Schram's time in hospital.

One morning, a senior officer called at my office. I soon realised that he wanted to talk, and it must have been a tremendous relief to be able to share some of his substantial problems with an outsider who was willing to listen.

There were problems in the chain of command and a tragic accident a week earlier had led to the death of a crew member, which had been devastating to the entire ship's company. Furthermore, the arrival of another senior officer's young and attractive daughter on board had seriously affected the studies and general behaviour of the eight cadets!

On visiting the ship, I had the opportunity to share my testimony with some of the cadets and to explain how the Lord had completely changed my life. Their training officer was also present, and I later had a chat with him in his cabin.

The following day, the training officer invited me and Rosemary to lunch on board, and before the ship sailed that evening – just five minutes before the gangway was taken up – I was able to take eight Flying Angel New Testaments on board for the eight cadets, containing the name of each cadet and a personal word of encouragement. I also gave the training officer several Christian books, which he seemed to appreciate.

Memorable ship visits
Around thirty-five parishioners and members of The Missions to Seamen Committee gathered in the clubroom one evening to view slides of Ethiopia and Israel by Captain Hare of the *MV Shoreham*. He had been a pilot on the Ethiopian coast for three years and had made friends with some American missionaries attached to the Red Sea Mission, so God was clearly speaking into his life.

On another occasion, we saw a Japanese flag flying down at Teesdock one morning. I had a chat with the captain and discovered that his daughter was attending a Methodist Mission School in Kobe. His parents were Buddhist, but when I asked him what he believed, he replied with a smile, "I am nothing." We organised a bus outing for twenty-one members of the crew and hosted sixteen of them at a social evening. It was a thoroughly enjoyable day for all involved.

In December 1970, the captain of the *MV Ribot* presented us with a magnificent four-decker Christmas cake as an expression of their appreciation for our hospitality. It was beautifully decorated and lit up by tiny light bulbs behind an elaborate network of icing.

In the January, we made one hundred and ninety-eight ship visits to seventy-eight vessels. An astonishing six hundred and thirty-five seamen visited Flying Angel House, and four hundred and thirty-three visited the onsite caravan, bringing the total to just shy of a thousand visitors!

We enjoyed entertaining the Mauritian crew of the *Belle Etoile* during their twelve days in port, and they shared how much they had welcomed the mission's hospitality during their previous visit, ten months earlier. One of the crew members asked me if we could have a time of prayer in the chapel one evening, and it was a pleasure to pray with and for him. At the request of other crew members, we arranged for a Roman Catholic priest to conduct Mass on board the ship.

This dockside opportunity in Wilton paved the way for me to take up an exciting new posting in Ceylon, heading up The Missions to Seamen there. Again, it was sad to say goodbye to our friends, but we knew that God was preparing us for the next chapter of our lives and were looking forward to a brand new adventure!

6. LIFE IN CEYLON

"You will receive power when the Holy Spirit comes on you; and you will be my witnesses...to the ends of the earth"

Acts 1:8

A pear-shaped island at the foot of India, Ceylon is about the same size as Ireland. Its history stretches back approximately two thousand five hundred years. It was conquered by the Portuguese during the sixteenth century and then by the Dutch, followed by the British. The Brits stuck around for a hundred and fifty years or so before Ceylon achieved independence in 1947. It became the Republic of Sri Lanka in 1972, while I was serving on the island.

Rosemary, Giles and I sailed out to Ceylon from England in July 1971, having joined The Missions to Seamen almost two years earlier, and we remained there until 1974. It was the most beautiful island we ever visited and, coinciding with the Cold War, it was a fascinating time to be there.

As the chaplain in charge of the 'Flying Angel Club', my main task was to visit ships of all nationalities in the port of Colombo. I was there to offer a warm welcome, to provide hospitality, and to arrange social and sporting activities for our visitors.

I was also tasked with distributing large volumes of Christian literature to anyone who was willing to accept it, and undertook a number of ship and hospital visits, not to mention attending countless parties on the ships with Rosemary and sometimes Giles in tow. We met a great many wonderful people and enjoyed their hospitality as well as offering plenty of hospitality ourselves. We helped to raise money for the mission through various social events and Rosemary's dedicated cardmaking endeavours.

I was also the part-time priest-in-charge at St Peter's Church near the harbour. I conducted a Holy Communion service each Sunday morning, and we often invited guests back to our flat for one of Rosemary's wonderful breakfasts afterwards. In addition, I held a midweek Communion service every Wednesday. We were delighted to invite many of the Christian seamen visiting Colombo to speak from the pulpit, including several from missionary ship the *Logos*, which docked in the port three times during our tenure in Ceylon.

The journey begins

The many adventures we experienced aboard our ship, the *Mahseer*, on our way over to Ceylon included a serious fire in the engine room between Gan Island and Colombo. The engines failed and the ship came to a grinding halt in the early hours one morning. It took half an hour, and all the ship's fire extinguishers and hoses, to bring the fire under control, the alarm bell sounding all the while.

Fire can be frightening in any circumstances, but when you're stuck on a ship with nowhere to go but down into the never-ending waves, it is utterly terrifying, Thankfully,

God had his hand upon us and nobody saw fit to launch me into the deep as in the case of Jonah! I had already experienced my five years in the belly of the large fish, albeit figuratively.

At Gan Island, we almost keeled over when the ship's anchor became entangled with an underwater cable attached to a gigantic block of concrete and hauled it to the surface. It looked as though we were scuppered, but thankfully gravity came to our aid and the useless hunk of additional cargo eventually released itself and returned to its original resting place.

It was a joy to be able to celebrate Holy Communion in the owner's suite, where Rosemary and I were staying, each Sunday morning. It sounds very grand, but it really wasn't! We had a number of officers present on each occasion, many of whom had never attended a church service before. I took the services as simply as possible and the number of attendees rose from Sunday to Sunday, eventually including the second engineers, second and third mates, and the mate. On one occasion, a force eight gale was raging, but despite the odd hand shooting out to steady the Communion table from time to time, we managed well.

One evening I decided to join the engineers on the eight-to-twelve watch and, duly clad in dazzling white overalls, I descended into the bowels of the ship. It proved a very interesting experience and, although somewhat soiled when I surfaced, I came up a far more enlightened padre! Until then I hadn't fully appreciated the level of claustrophobia the crew faced and the harsh conditions they had to endure as they went about their work. It was an eye-opening experience.

We made various stop-offs along the way, including one in Amsterdam with Padre Andrews, who was very kind, and one in Durban with Padre Wilson-Hughes, who was incredibly hospitable. It was great to break up our voyage, which took around six weeks, and to be back on dry land for a few days.

At the age of six, Giles enjoyed every minute of the journey over and was thoroughly spoilt by the officers. He even had his hair cut by the ship's barber one day. We were the only passengers on board, so he had the run of the ship and would be taken off by various members of the crew to help with some job or other, invariably returning to us covered in muck!

Our first impression of Colombo

After our long, rough and eventful voyage, Rosemary, Giles and I were relieved and excited to see the twinkling lights of Colombo on August 16, 1971. The following morning, Mr Dixon-Clarke and Mr Abayekoon came on board and warmly welcomed us to Colombo. However, it took us a while to get through customs, who searched all but one of our thirty-seven pieces of luggage, with the exception of Rosemary's handbag!

Once on land, it soon became apparent that the mission in Colombo was facing serious financial difficulties, with a good deal of outstanding credit to repay. Our mission in Ceylon was to offer hope and refuge to visiting seamen, but our predecessors seemed to have been so far up to their necks in 'beer and skittles' that our goal of sharing the gospel with visitors to Colombo was in serious jeopardy. This resulted in a difficult decision to sell one of the mission's motorboats, *Stuart C Knox III*.

Furthermore, the chaplain's car was literally falling to pieces. One day as I was leaving the docks, I was flagged down by a Sinhalese man who handed me part of my bumper, which had fallen off on the way in. The speedometer didn't work and the repair bill for work undertaken a full year earlier hadn't been paid.

Months later, the car's steering mechanism failed, and thankfully we were on a level road rather than on a mountain track or the outcome might have been quite different. It was the eve of the Buddhist New Year, so all the local businesses were closed, and the local official told us that wild elephants had caused considerable damage in the area a night or so before. He kindly invited us back to his hut and plied us with local delicacies. Throughout the night, local Sinhalese turned up one after another to bring us gifts of bananas, oil cakes and milk rice. We were very touched by their kindness and generosity.

By 'coincidence', the owner of the nearest garage – around five miles away – just happened to be driving past at one o'clock the following morning. He alighted from his lorry and immediately set to work by torchlight. He continued until three o'clock, at which point he had to return to his garage to retrieve some equipment, but he was back within a few hours to finish the job. Our good Samaritan returned with sweet tea for us and proceeded to work in the blistering sun until the car was fixed up.

Social and sporting endeavours

We had plenty of visitors to entertain and appointments to attend during our three-year tenure. Five officers from the *Mahseer* arrived for Holy Communion the Sunday after we disembarked. We invited them for breakfast after the service, but just as they lifted their knives and forks they were summoned back to the ship as there had been a total power failure on board!

Later that day, the crew from the *Mahseer* – including yours truly – took on the crew from the *Chilka*, whom we had befriended, in a game of football. Despite our best efforts, we lost five nil. This was the first of many friendly matches between the crews of various vessels, which were almost invariably followed by parties aboard one of the ships.

One month, eight football matches took place and two hundred and thirty-six seamen were involved, either as players or spectators. I was injured during one match and ended up with a poisoned leg, which landed me in bed for three days with a temperature and a leg that resembled a tree trunk!

We also arranged a number of tennis matches with members of various ships, which helped me keep up with some of the athletic endeavours of my younger years. Later during our stay, I was honoured to present Flying Angel pennants at the Royal Colombo Yacht Club to the winners and runners-up of the annual Missions to Seamen Race.

Another time, I arranged a cricket match between a team from the *Carpenteria* and a local air force team. I also organised a basketball match for some Filipino shipmates at one time and a badminton tournament for a group of Indian seamen at another. I was so grateful to God that I was able to continue with some of my beloved sporting activities, albeit in a very different setting.

I also decided to join the squash ladder at the old Queen's Club, as I had found it to be an excellent way of keeping fit. I was fortunate to escape conclusive defeat and a fatal fall from the ladder when I came up against a most unexpected opponent one evening. My friend and I had just left the court when the marker suddenly became excited and pointed to something on the ground close to our feet.

On cautiously approaching the spot, we saw a small snake curled up near the entrance, which the marker emphatically assured us was a tic polonga (a Russell's viper), one of Ceylon's deadliest snakes. An admirable spirit of self-preservation overwhelming his Buddhist scruples, he quickly terminated its sporting inclinations with the help of an iron bar, to our considerable relief. The marker spoke very little English, but through a series of noises and gestures he managed to convey the fact that a European man had been killed by a tic polonga at the same squash courts twenty years earlier.

Later on, Rosemary and I climbed to the top of Adam's Peak, a holy mountain that stretches up to 7,359 feet (2,243 metres), and is revered by Muslims, Hindus and Buddhists. We were the only English climbers at that time, though a few hundred from other cultures were making the attempt, and chanting as they went. From a distance, the peak looked impossible to climb, but there are steps cut into the rock that went all the way around it. We had to go round and round to get to the top, but it was well worth it once we got there. I think that's a great analogy for the Christian life, which takes twists and turns but is infinitely worth it once you reach the summit!

Rosemary was just as busy as I was in Colombo, playing host and cooking for the many people who came and went, and making around four hundred birthday and Christmas cards one year to support the mission financially. The proceeds were put towards the redecoration of the mission building – including the billiard room and jewellery shop – which I undertook myself.

In addition to my numerous speaking engagements, Rosemary spoke about the work of the mission at several meetings, including at a gathering of the clergy wives. On another occasion, she spoke to approximately thirty ladies from the United Nations.

Interesting contacts

While visiting the British High Commission, we met a Miss Frank who worked there. It transpired that she hailed from Lazenby, Teeside, and I had presided over her niece's wedding the previous year. Miss Frank had been at school with Winifred Walker, our organist at Wilton, and I had visited her aged father during our time there. Despite being thousands of miles away, it turned out to be a much smaller world than we had realised!

Another interesting contact we made was with the Dutch captain of a Singaporean ship. Three months earlier, the ship he was master of had sprung a leak in the middle of the Bay of Bengal and started to sink. The captain and his all-Chinese crew had taken to the two lifeboats.

Sixteen blisteringly hot days later – his legs were subsequently bandaged from his feet to his thighs – the first lifeboat was washed up on the Burmese coast, some seven hundred and fifty miles from the shipwrecked vessel. Three men had died in that boat, probably more through a lack of opium than food, while five had died on the other boat, which had been washed ashore many miles further south the previous day.

The captain had experienced some sort of encounter with God during the journey, and had subsequently been dragged by his Norwegian wife to a Christian convention organised by the Fountain Trust in Guildford, much against his will. During his two weeks in port at Colombo, we shared several meals and I had the opportunity to give him some Christian literature, including a copy of John's Gospel.

Another time, I boarded a Filipino ship, the *Matlas Explorer*, to present the entire ship's company with Christmas cards containing a small financial contribution from their friends at St Peter's Church and the Missions to Seamen. I had visited the ship six months previously, and it had been stranded in port since then with a hardening cargo of cement that hadn't been sold.

The crew were missing their families and the embassy had tried to fly them home, but they were deeply worried that they wouldn't be paid their wages if they simply abandoned the ship. I later learnt that the ship had finally sailed to Dubai with its cargo and that the crew members had been told they would be paid in full on their arrival.

In February 1972, I met the captain of a Romanian ship and visited him several times subsequently. I presented him with a Flying Angel New Testament, which he seemed pleased to accept. Although he didn't wish me to broadcast the fact, he confided to me that his uncle was the president of Romania, the infamous Nicolae Ceausescu!

I also met an interesting man named Norman who had been converted in a manner not unlike my own. The 49-year-old British engineer had been glued to the television in the officers' bar watching the Munich Olympics. A young cadet named Martin was being ragged for ordering an orange juice, but Norman was too focused on the athletics to pay much attention. Then, suddenly, a single sentence, uttered with confidence by Martin, rang out across the crowded bar and hit Norman like a bolt of electricity. The words were: "Yes, sir, but you see I know Jesus Christ."

Norman immediately lost interest in the Olympics and turned his attention to the young cadet. He gave his heart to the Lord shortly afterwards at a Christian meeting, but it was Martin's bold witness and the subsequent conversations they had about the Lord that led to Norman's conversion.

Norman's life was completely transformed as a result. Once a heavy drinker, he gave up alcohol for good and his changed life had a profound impact on his fellow officers. I had the pleasure of taking some Christian books aboard for Norman and praying with him. His story reminded me afresh of the simple power of the gospel. All we need do is speak the name of Jesus and lives can be changed for all eternity.

While a curfew and austerity measures were in place during some of our time in the country, we were able to host various special events, including our 8 Bells Ball in 1972, which had been cancelled due to these restrictions the year before. It was a wonderful occasion, enjoyed by all one hundred and fifty guests, and it continued on until three thirty in the morning! It also enabled us to raise a considerable sum in advertising revenue from local firms, which was invested straight back into the mission.

Our 1972 carol service was well attended, with eleven officers from the *Carpentaria* enjoying the festivities. The captain and second engineer read two of the lessons and around fifteen seamen were present in total. Rosemary sang carols with the Colombo Philharmonic Choir in a performance at the cathedral while Giles and I took part in the accompanying pageant. I took the part of Joseph and Giles was page to King Caspar.

Key events
Rosemary, Giles and I attended a birthday party aboard the *MV Julunga* one evening, and the following day the second engineer, along with his wife and two children, joined us for lunch. On another occasion, we hosted the

wife of the electrician, Garry Scott, from the *Manipur*, who stayed with us while her husband was in hospital with hepatitis. Garry had sailed out with us on the *Mahseer*, so we were glad to be in a position to help them in their time of need.

We attended the consecration of Cyral Abeynaike as the tenth bishop of Colombo at St Thomas' College, Mount Lavinia. The open-air service was colourful and impressive, attracting a crowd of around two-and-a-half thousand people. Despite an impromptu downpour, the service was an incredible blend of Eastern and Western cultures, with lively music and readings in English, Sinhalese and Tamil. The following evening, I attended the enthronement of the bishop at the Cathedral Church of Christ.

We arranged trips for numerous international crews, including an excursion to Kandy with fifteen Italians and a trip to the nearest zoo with five West Africans. One particular highlight for us was the Esala Perahera in Kandy, which featured seventy gorgeously apparelled elephants in addition to dancers, drummers, musicians and acrobats proceeding through the streets, which were lit by flaming torches. It was a magnificent spectacle. We attended the festival with a coachload of people including seven East Germans, one British officer and one Dane.

The visit of our general secretary, Revd Tom Kerfoot, to Colombo was another wonderful occasion, and he stayed with us for three days. During this time, Tom, along with Mr Lawrence (our chairman) and I, were granted an interview with the President of the Republic, who seemed pleased that we were in the country as Christian ministers.

I officiated at several funerals during my time in Ceylon, including that of one of our part-time sidesmen at the municipal cemetery. He was a true Christian and the joyous message of the resurrection rang out in the prayers, readings and hymns. I estimated that around two hundred people attended on that occasion.

The funeral that most sticks in my mind was that of Ronald MacDonnell, the Canadian high commissioner to Ceylon, who had died suddenly of a heart attack at the age of sixty-four. He was a real believer, and although I never had the pleasure of meeting him, his family and friends had no doubt that he had gone straight to heaven, which was a great comfort to them. He had travelled all over the world, including a stint at Oxford University as well as serving as an ambassador to Egypt and Lebanon.

The senior 'free church' British minister had been living in Ceylon for around twenty-five years. He just happened to be away on home leave in Scotland at this time, so muggins here found himself in a very difficult position. I assisted Rev Celestine Fernando, general secretary of the Ceylon Bible Society and a great friend of ours, with the funeral preparations, and was asked to give an address at the memorial service. The church was packed with ambassadors and diplomats, as well as senior representatives from the Ceylon government. It was one of those tasks one finds oneself called to do in faraway places in the Lord's service!

Having only attended one memorial service in my life, it was an altogether novel experience for me but, with the vital help of the Holy Spirit, I felt very uninhibited in the pulpit. I was able to speak of our wonderful Lord Jesus and to share Mr MacDonnell's confident assurance that he had gone directly into the arms of the Lord when he died.

Some of those in attendance were from Communist countries, so it was amazing that I had the opportunity to speak so freely into their lives in a way that would not normally have been permitted for them. I was nervous, but the Lord strengthens us for such occasions and I strongly felt his presence with me. I later received a lovely letter from Mrs MacDonnell, with a donation for the mission enclosed.

With no British ships in dock over the Christmas 1973, we decided not to hold our 8 Bells Ball, but to host a benefit film show instead. We invited a number of guests to a screening of *Scrooge* at one of the local cinemas, including the British High Commissioner and his wife, Mrs Smedley. We hosted around three hundred and eighty people at the Christmas service, although only a handful were seamen.

Sometime after that, Rosemary and I were invited to Westminster House for cocktails along with around twelve hundred other guests. The event was hosted by the British High Commissioner and Mrs Smedley to celebrate the Queen's official birthday. We were very honoured to be invited by the Head of Chancery to accompany him into the drawing room in order to meet the Prime Minister, Sirimavo Bandaranaike, who served as Prime Minister of Ceylon and Sri Lanka three times, and was the modern world's first female head of government. Rosemary and I sat either side of her and chatted quite informally for a few minutes.

I also arranged a trip for Giles' class to be shown around a ship named *The City of Montreal*. He came home full of stories about everything he had seen. I wondered whether we had a future seaman on our hands, as he had never lost his love for ship life from the journey over. Later during our time in Ceylon, Giles sailed to Galle on the *Logos*. He enjoyed the adventure immensely!

Most importantly of all, Giles gave his heart to the Lord in his Sunday school in Colombo when he was about seven or eight. I was delighted to hear that, as this is surely the greatest gift you can give your children. He has followed the Lord ever since and is determined to leave the same legacy for Anna and Samuel.

Happy holidays

In August 1973, Rosemary, Giles and I flew to Madras for an unforgettable three-week holiday in India and Nepal. The Lord had provided in an amazing way and we were so grateful for his goodness to us. It was the first time Rosemary and Giles had ever flown, so that was exciting in itself!

During our travels, we went to see Rosemary's birthplace in North India, which was quite an emotional time for her. There was an old man who had heard about our coming and had travelled from a long way away on foot to meet Rosemary, whom he remembered as a child. She was very moved by his visit. We also visited a snake pit, which reminded me of my earlier encounter on the squash courts, and Giles enjoyed a ride on an elephant.

On the little plane between Patna and Kathmandu, I sat next to a chap on the plane and noticed that before we took off he bowed his head, closed his eyes and his lips were moving. I also noticed that he muttered grace before eating the snacks that were duly handed out. That was enough to get us talking, and I soon realised he was a Christian.

When we got to Kathmandu, we shared a taxi from the airport. On the way to meet our friends, this man said, "Do you mind if we stop off? There's a chap I know who's an Anglican priest and his church is nearby."

He introduced me to this friend of his, Revd Attialy and his family, and he asked if I would like to preach for him on the Sunday, which was just a few days away. I didn't have any books or materials with me as we were on holiday, but I offered to give my testimony. It was funny because the organist didn't turn up on the day, so Rosemary ended up playing the organ!

Brian Sennett, one of the four white people who attended the service and a teacher at a Roman Catholic school, came up to me afterwards and said he had been most interested to hear about my conversion. He knew Julian Charley well and had also run with him many years earlier. It was funny to think that somebody in this little church in Kathmandu could be connected to the man who had first introduced me to Jesus.

Even more amazingly, there were two Canadian women at the service and one of them, Miss Bell, asked the name of the person I had met on the train crossing Canada, whom I had mentioned during my testimony. I said that her name was Annie Ferguson, not expecting there to be any connection given the size of the country, but it turned out this lady knew her personally! I found that quite astonishing, and once again it reminded me that the Christian world is small and beautifully interwoven.

The night before we had left for Nepal, we had prayed that we would be able to enjoy some Christian fellowship while we were away, and the very morning of our departure we had received a letter from Dick and Bev Young, who had been on the *Logos* but were living in northeast India at this point. They had just opened a bookshop, so we were able to stay with them for a couple of nights. Giles was delighted to find that they had a mound of books for him to devour, so he promptly sat himself down on the floor and was happily occupied for hours.

We enjoyed spending time with the team and attended an evening prayer meeting during our stay. The following day, I was asked to share my testimony, which I was happy to do, as always. I was later approached by two members of the team who wanted to hear more, and it was a great encouragement to me to be able to tell them of the Lord's goodness to us. Afterwards, we visited Swayambhunath, the monkey temple, which Giles particularly loved, and the Chobhar Gorge, an area of outstanding natural beauty.

Extra special visitors
We were delighted to welcome our younger daughter, Jane, to Colombo for a period of three months. During her stay, we took a week's holiday and travelled up to Nuwara Eliya, a city in the tea and hill country of central Ceylon, where we sat around a huge log fire in the evenings to keep warm. While visiting the Sea Anglers' Club at Trincomalee afterwards, we frequently had to jump into the sea to cool off! It was our first holiday in more than six months and we found our relaxing stay in the mountains a great tonic.

Our older daughter, Lin, flew out to join us in Colombo shortly after this, as did my parents, who were on their way back from a stay in New Zealand with my brother Jeremy and his family. They were among the fifty guests who came to a special parish breakfast we hosted at the Missions to Seamen. Mrs Sirimanne provided a delicious meal of curry and string hoppers, and it was a very happy occasion.

Another particularly special time for us was the return of the *Logos* in March 1972, complete with tons of educational and Christian books. The one hundred and thirty people on board originated from twenty-two countries and were all committed Christians, serving as volunteers for years at a time within this marvellous ministry, some with their whole families. Their chief aim was to spread the good news of Jesus in every way possible.

I visited the ship at least once a day while it was in port and got to know many of the young people on board. Every so often, someone would sing the opening bars of a hymn or chorus and then others, both aboard and ashore if they were in earshot, would join in. That was so special. They had a packed programme while they were in Colombo and many lives were touched by the work of Operation Mobilisation during their time with us.

One Sunday, I invited the chief engineer, who originally hailed from Texas, to speak at our Communion service, and the following week I invited a junior engineer from Australia to give his testimony. We also had the privilege of inviting the director of Operation Mobilisation, George Verwer, to speak at St Peter's one Sunday. His words were profound, challenging and inspiring in equal measure.

We invited crew members back to our flat for breakfast after the Sunday Communion service each week as well as organising a trip to a rubber estate for some of the children and families on board, which they thoroughly enjoyed. It was quite a moving experience standing on the quayside with a large crowd when the time came to wave off these precious Christians from so many lands.

The *Logos* visited Ceylon again in March 1973. Another twelve special days of fellowship and ministry that I will never forget followed. The vessel's public relations officer stayed with us for five weeks, having come ahead of the ship in order to make preparations for the stopover in Colombo. His assistant arrived a week after this and we were also able to put him up.

Once again, it was a joy to meet the crew and see the many great things they were able to accomplish through their packed programme, united in their love and devotion to Jesus Christ. On three occasions, we invited friends from the ship to our flat to meet with some of our local friends. There were between fifteen and twenty people present on each of these evenings and it was precious to hear the testimonies of our *Logos* friends, which were given in word and song.

One of the highlights of the visit was an embassy reception on board the ship, attended by a number of East European diplomats, including the Russian ambassador and his first secretary. I shook hands with the first secretary and had a brief chat with him after the meal.

We were entertained by some of the *Logos* singers and guitarists, and by Lylie Godridge and his singers. These performances gave a wonderful testimony to the risen Lord and were compounded by an inspiring talk from George Verwer at the end of the evening. He spoke with such charm and tact, yet managed to convey the message of God's great love in such a powerful way.

Each guest was offered a beautifully bound edition of *The Living Bible* free of charge as we left the room. When I chatted to my new Russian friend shortly afterwards, he confided in me that, not only had he accepted a copy, but that he also had a Russian translation at home.

Sometime earlier, we had invited the Russian assistant military, air and naval attaché and his wife to a small supper party, and in return we were invited to a party at their home. I had a long discussion with him and was able to speak on the subject of Christianity vis-à-vis Communism.

Another monumental visit was that of Revd John Stott, the rector of All Souls, Langham Place in London, and chaplain to the Queen. He gave a series of seminars and theological lectures at a large local church, which were very well attended by pastors, clergy and laymen from various denominations.

I was invited to a luncheon with John Stott by the local director of Every Home Crusade, and it was wonderful to spend time with this great scholar and humble man of God. I was also able to tell him that Julian Charley, the man who first introduced me to Jesus, had always aspired to become one of John Stott's chaplains. He had achieved his goal by this point and John Stott seemed delighted to hear that Julian had been so instrumental in my conversion.

Visiting the sick and afflicted

We visited many seamen who had been hospitalised for one reason or another. A Polish man had lost all the fingers on his right hand while handling some explosive charge at sea, and an older English gentleman had a severe compound fracture in his right leg following a serious accident at sea. We discovered that an Italian seaman who was staying in the same hospital with a minor injury had been a prisoner of war in Wales for most of the Second World War. He had married a Welsh lady and, when not at sea, they lived in Naples with their growing family.

During one hospital visit, I had the privilege of meeting Captain Tan from Taiwan. He suffered from bilharzia, which causes severe internal bleeding. He was a committed Christian and had a Chinese New Testament with him. I discovered that he had almost been shipwrecked fifteen years earlier, and some of the crew had leapt overboard to their deaths, but his prayers had been answered when an American ship picked up his distress signals and came to their aid in the nick of time.

We visited a Goanese seaman on one occasion who had been stabbed in the stomach while he slept by a fellow seaman who had experienced a breakdown in mental health. He had been at the hospital for several weeks and was expected to remain there for some time. I presented him with a New Testament and he read it to the exclusion of anything else.

Another time, I visited Fraser Nursing Home to see a young cadet named Robert, a devoted Christian, who had fallen fifteen to twenty feet from the bridge of the *Clan Malcolm*. He had narrowly avoided falling a further twenty-five feet into the bottom of the hold, and it was a miracle that he wasn't killed. I was touched to hear that his non-Christian colleague, the ship's second mate, had sat by his bedside for two hours after the accident, reading the Bible to him.

On Christmas Day in 1972, Rosemary and I visited eleven seamen in the local hospitals and presented each with a small gift from the mission. The following year, we visited five hospitalised seamen, presenting them with a Christmas card and a box of tea from the mission, which they gratefully received.

While recovering from my own poisoned leg incident, I visited an elderly lady on the outskirts of Colombo who believed an evil spell had been cast upon her. I had experienced a similar encounter in East Africa, and in both cases unexplained phenomena had occurred. We prayed together and fortunately she experienced no further trouble.

Preparing to leave

Shortly before we returned to the UK, Rosemary, Giles and I visited the Ekston Rubber Estate at Puwakpitiya, as I had been asked to speak at a Lenten cottage meeting that evening. As the following day was a Poya Day, a national holiday, we spent it relaxing with some friends in their lovely garden, which was an ideal spot for birdwatching.

As well as saying goodbye to the many wonderful friends we had made in Colombo and the surrounding area, we realised we would be unable to return to England with our two pet chipmunks in tow. They were taken off our hands by a group of Dutch officers in exchange for a generous donation to the mission. Giles was particularly sad to say goodbye to them.

Before we left, we spent a week's holiday at the Yala Game Reserve in the south of the island, which was marvellous. We flew back to the UK, eager to see our friends and family. However, we all had the feeling that this wouldn't be our sole overseas mission, and that God had plenty more adventures in store for us.

7. THE DEVIL OF AMSTERDAM

"Submit yourselves, then, to God. Resist the devil, and he will flee from you."

James 4:7

Following our travels around India, we returned to the UK in the summer of 1974 and it was wonderful to be reunited with Lin, Jane and all our other friends and family. We spent a further six months with the Missions to Seamen in Gravesend, at which point I started looking for opportunities elsewhere. I made enquiries through the Church Pastoral Aid Society and heard there was a vacancy with the Commonwealth and Continental Church Society (which became the Intercontinental Church Society) for an Anglican chaplain at Christ Church Amsterdam.

I went for an interview, and one of the things that impressed me immediately was that the interviewer said, "Brian, let's pray about this." This hadn't been the protocol at The Missions to Seamen and I instinctively felt, "This is right. God is in this."

Little did I know that a tangible spiritual battle was raging in the city and it would be the most difficult assignment of our lives. As I look back now, I thank God for bringing us through it and for everything I learnt while we were there, even though some of the lessons were pretty tough to take on board.

The early days

We set sail from Harwich to the Hook of Holland on New Year's Day 1975, and I was inducted into the church on the Saturday evening of January 4. I was delighted to see such a large congregation in attendance and to be warmly welcomed by so many of the church members. However, I soon realised that this new role would be far from plain sailing. It transpired that I was about to be handed a hornet's nest.

My predecessor had been working out in Africa for many years, but hadn't been ordained until quite late in his life. He was very high church and not a nice man at all. From the very beginning, I felt there was a strong force rising up against me, and he played a major part in it, although I eventually realised that it went way beyond this man and his merry band of followers.

Quite soon after we arrived, we spoke to a lovely Christian lady who lived right behind the church building and became a dear friend of ours. Her name was Lys van der Bom, but she was affectionately known as Lys 'Ban der Bomb'. I found out later that she and her sister had hidden several Jews in their home during the war.

Rosemary was president of the Ladies' Association and Lys served as vice-president, and they were a great blessing to one another. Lys was very aware of the problems that had been going on, which had been kept secret from many of the other church members, and she confided in us about some very concerning issues. We later discovered that everything she had told us was true, and we often prayed together when things got tough.

The outgoing minister had lived in the flat above the church, where Rosemary, Giles and I were to live. We soon learnt that he had been hypnotising members of the congregation outside the scheduled church services and had built up quite a following. He was also having a long-term affair with the choir mistress, who was some thirty years his junior. I gathered he had a certain amount of charm and quite a musical talent.

The choir mistress had lived in the same flat, at the other end of the long corridor from this minister and his wife. It was just a yard or two away from a door leading directly into our upstairs 'church room'. He would leave his wife in their bed and go down the passageway to the spare room, and it was fairly likely that the wife knew about it. I found it all very strange.

This room became Giles', and on one occasion he complained about not sleeping well when he was there at the weekends, which was unusual for a child. During that week, Rosemary and I prayed against any evil presence in that room, although we knew nothing of the goings-on at the time. From then on, Giles had no trouble sleeping.

Another immediate struggle when we arrived was that word had got around that I was an evangelical, and the church wasn't at all evangelical. We sensed the antipathy from among my predecessor's followers straightaway. I also felt that some members were particularly keen on academic distinction, and it got around to one or two that I had an old Oxford tie. I still wore the tie on occasion, but they felt this was deceitful as I hadn't passed my exams. As they already had it in for me, they were clutching at straws to find out anything they could about the new man, and a group of people soon rose up in arms against me.

Giles was nine at this time and he attended The British School in the Netherlands in The Hague. He boarded there with Revd John Lewis, his wife Ann and their four boys, Jonathan, Christopher, Sam and George. Rosemary would take him there early on Monday morning and collect him after school on Friday. John was chaplain at The Hague at the time and was a tremendous help and encouragement to us. He later wrote a book called *Something Happened at The Hague*, which was his account of how the Lord blessed them all there. It made for a very interesting read.

During our time in Amsterdam, we imported our Sri Lankan cat, Little Tigger. She was flown over in a jumbo jet at huge expense. Quite how much only became apparent on arrival at Amsterdam Airport Schiphol, and the airline offered to fly her back if we refused to pay!

I retorted, "But that will cost you twice as much!"

A price was eventually agreed and she became probably the first ever Sri Lankan cat to live in Western Europe, eventually expiring in Lyon!

As an aside, this wasn't her only adventure. Years earlier she had survived a fall of sixty feet from our balcony in Colombo, having taken a swipe at a crow, we think! Little Tigger had also enjoyed chasing the chipmunks we had then around the sitting room, but she never attacked them. Whenever they stopped moving, she would simply freeze and stare at them!

Trouble in the ranks

My first choir practice as the new incumbent was conducted by the choir mistress in Dutch. They knew that I was brand new in the country and spoke no Dutch at all, while they could all speak perfect English and the services were always conducted in English. I felt that was pretty strange and told her afterwards, in no uncertain terms, that choir practices were to be conducted in English from then on.

The next practice was conducted in English, but the pressure continued to build and the first few months were very difficult. A lot of people in the congregation knew that things hadn't been right under my predecessor and I sensed their support, but things soon came to a head with the forty-two-member choir, most of whom were close followers of the former minister and the choir mistress. The choir had achieved international acclaim and would travel to different countries, including the UK, to perform, but I came to realise that it was one of the strongholds that needed to be brought down.

The time came when I heard God's voice almost audibly for the first time. I was walking into the church behind the choir procession and prayed, "Lord, you know exactly what's going on. I feel out of my depth. Please show me what to do."

When he responded, I knew it was God's voice because he used language that he had used some two thousand years ago when he was on earth, and besides that it was language that I wouldn't have normally used. He said, "Brian, I want you to cleanse my temple." What a thrilling and unforgettable experience! What peace and boldness it gave me!

I stood up in the pulpit and said, "Many of you know that there are lots of things going on in the church that aren't right. I feel that God wants to do something about this. With effect from the end of this service, I'm disbanding the choir."

A moment of deafening silence gave way to complete pandemonium! The choir secretary had a genuine asthmatic fit and was carried out. She had been very much in league with the others. Another man stormed out of the church and then realised he had left behind his son, who was a treble in the choir, so he stormed back in, grabbed him and dragged him out. Another woman loudly burst into tears and made her feelings very clear.

Despite this shocking disruption, we had to continue the service. It came to the next hymn, and I felt instinctively that the people who had stayed were behind me, simply by the way they sang it. There was a vigour that hadn't been there before and, despite the uproar my words had caused, I knew that God was about to start turning the situation around.

It was amazing how rapidly things happened after that. News got around about what was going on, even reaching the shores of England. To begin with, I started to receive notes from the wardens after they had collected the offerings. These notes had been put into the collection by people who wanted to tell me, in secret, that they had been praying for an intervention for a long time and that they were thankful to God for bringing me to the church.

There were also notes of strong opposition, but it was a relief to know that many of the people were on the same page as me. Then letters began arriving from England to the effect that people had been very concerned about the church, and particularly the behaviour of the choir, and had been praying for change for some time.

The situation really started to improve after a young Dutchman suggested that we start meeting for a midweek prayer session in addition to our regular Bible study meetings. We set the time for six thirty on a Wednesday morning and invited people to come along. Rosemary kindly agreed to cook breakfast afterwards, which helped us get to know our prayer partners pretty well.

Many people faithfully rode their bikes there in all weathers and from quite a distance, and praying together made all the difference. We regularly had nine or ten people in attendance, and on one occasion I counted eighteen. It was great to have that support and we began to feel a real sense of unity among us. The more we prayed, the more we felt that the strongholds were beginning to come down. Over time, we saw many miracles occur. Never underestimate the power of prayer!

Around this time, I had a remarkable dream. I was embroiled in a life-threatening struggle with an evil spirit on the edge of a very steep cliff. I found myself looking down and I could see the sea crashing against the rocks below me. I was vomiting profusely and could see a lot of blood flowing out of me. In that moment of intense danger, I felt strongly that I had won the battle through the deliverance of my heavenly Father. I woke up full of thanks and woke Rosemary to tell her of the breakthrough dream.

I later received an interpretation of the dream from an evangelist named John Rawlings. The interpretation matched my feelings about it and confirmed that the dream was indeed from God. During the same meeting, Rosemary received the laying on of hands for the baptism of the Spirit and spoke in tongues. It was a momentous occasion and one that encouraged us both greatly in our faith and mission.

On another occasion, a demonic presence entered our bedroom in a physical form. It placed its hands around my throat, strangling me so that I couldn't breathe. I was unable to speak or fight it off. Rosemary woke up and saw what was happening, and banished the spirit in the name of Jesus. The demon vanished, and I was able to breathe again. Afterwards, there were marks on my neck where it had tried to strangle me, bearing testament to the event and to the fact that my darling wife had saved my life by calling on the name of the Lord.

The devil comes to steal, kill and destroy, but Jesus gives us truly abundant life!

Red lights and demons

When people visit Amsterdam, they are often taken on tours of the infamous red-light district, which was just a stone's throw from the church. It was impossible to ignore the many sex shops, gambling dens and brothels. Virtually naked prostitutes sat in ground floor windows day and night, beckoning their clients in. It was truly a modern-day Sodom and Gomorrah.

Despite this, there was a wonderful work for the Lord going on behind the railway station, where a couple of house boats had been moored together. This ministry was run by the leader of YWAM in Amsterdam. He was about six foot seven and quite formidable-looking. One Sunday I invited him to speak at Christ Church and it was valuable to hear someone who knew the perils of the red-light district first hand and was willing to publicly denounce the sins of the city as he spoke openly about the situation. There was an awful hullabaloo about it afterwards when it was reported to the bishop by the 'gang', primarily because he hadn't worn a cassock.

On one occasion, my predecessor, who had been told very clearly by the bishop that he must not come near the church, turned up with some of his trusty followers in tow. This man had told members of the disbanded choir to keep quiet at certain times and then to suddenly start singing at inopportune moments during the service. It was very disruptive, but we did our best to ignore them.

Around this time, the Lord brought all sorts of people to the weekly prayer meeting. One girl wearing a veil turned up straight from working at a nightclub. She hadn't specifically come for the meeting, but she clearly needed help and we invited her to come back for a time of prayer another day. It took about five hours for the whole prayer team to come against the evil spirits inhabiting this young woman, and we commanded that they leave her in Jesus' name.

It was quite a dramatic moment when the breakthrough finally came. We heard a deep male voice bellowing out of this quite attractive young woman, and a growling noise as the demons came out of her. Afterwards, her voice returned to normal and she was back to being herself once again.

After this encounter, I quickly had to start learning about exorcising evil spirits as many others living in and frequenting the red-light district were afflicted by them. I was an absolute beginner, so I read many books and asked for advice from others who knew more on the subject.

On another occasion, Rosemary was up in the flat when a transvestite came and asked to speak me. He was an Oxford graduate and had heard about the work I had been doing while attending the well-known English church nearby. This man was also being bothered by evil spirits, so I prayed for him in my study that he might have the victory over them in Jesus' name, taking authority over every power and principality that was attacking him. He was soon grovelling around on the ground as the spirits tried to resist, and the demonic presence in the room was very real.

Rosemary heard all sorts of groans, screams and funny noises as the demons responded to my prayers. She wondered what was happening to me and even became a little concerned, running down the steep stairs to check that I was OK! I finished praying for him once I was confident that the demons had left his body. He was truly grateful because there was no ministry for casting out demons at the other church, and he had experienced a real encounter with God. He occasionally attended Christ Church, and thankfully he remained free from demonic oppression from that day forth.

Shocking news

On March 22, 1979, the British ambassador to the Netherlands, Sir Richard Sykes, was assassinated, along with his Dutch footman. The news came as quite a shock as we had been well-acquainted, and we sent flowers for the funeral on behalf of the congregation. I also wrote to Lady Sykes expressing our deep sympathy for her loss and that of her three grown-up children, assuring her of our prayers.

Rosemary and I were among the fifteen hundred or so people to be invited to the memorial service at The Hague, which was a sombre affair. We live in a sinful world and the only way to overcome this sin is through the blood of Jesus. This and other terrible events that took place at around this time – including the assassination of shadow Northern Ireland secretary, Airey Neave – reminded us of the importance of prayer and of speaking out about Jesus at every opportunity.

Personal attacks

Living so close to the red-light district, I had to be very careful myself. By the grace of God, I never went off the rails, but I was tempted in various ways while we were in Amsterdam. There were negative influences all around us, and as the church leader I was severely under attack. It was particularly difficult for Rosemary, as some of the women weren't at all shy in trying to seduce me, and that was just members of the congregation! Again, it was the prayers of the faithful that helped me stay on track.

I was reliant on the Holy Spirit to help me when things got tough and took practical measures, such as ensuring that other people were present when I was ministering to women on their own. That offered an immediate protection from the devil's attacks, because ultimately that's what they were.

Furthermore, the church was being infiltrated by a cult called the Invisible Church, the members of which made themselves very visible indeed. They openly came into the church and tried to draw people away from it. The church treasurer also caused us many problems and false accusations against me began to pour in from various factions, which was an obvious attempt on the devil's part to try to get rid of me.

The level of dissent grew and eventually the news reached England via letters of accusation sent by members of the church to the bishop. An extraordinary church meeting was arranged via London and a senior cleric was sent to preside over it in place of the bishop himself.

Thirty-two of our church members had signed a motion of no confidence in me as chaplain. To my horror, thirteen accusations were read out against me at the meeting. The majority were entirely untrue, while others had been framed in such a way as to convey a very serious distortion of the truth. While I was always ready to admit my various faults and failings, my conscience before God was clear with regard to each and every one, and many were later proved to be quite false. These accusations related to fairly minor complaints, such as my reluctance to baptise the children of parents who were not remotely believers.

I felt my accusers were trying to tarnish my reputation, but I knew that it was my duty as chaplain to protect my flock – and even those standing against me – as best I could. Therefore, I refrained from defending myself even when I could easily have done so to avoid further unpleasantness. Instead, I left the situation in God's capable hands and allowed him to vindicate me over time. Whatever you are going through right now, and however impossible the situation appears, trust in him. He is always good and ever faithful.

It had come as a great shock to us as a couple to hear these criticisms read out in public and to know that there was such animosity against me, but again I thank God for bringing us through the hard times and covering us in his peace and love. Around one hundred and thirty others attended the meeting, including some from different churches, and there was such great support from them that my accusers were silenced. Praise be to God! Many letters were sent from our parishioners to the bishop denying the accusations and supporting me, and I was so grateful to those who upheld me.

I thank the Lord for my wonderful wife, who stood by my side at all times and gave me such incredible support. Rosemary was adored, and rightly so. She was just marvellous. As we really wanted to get to know our flock outside the services, Rosemary started hosting a breakfast after the Sunday service, and that created a great time of fellowship for all who came. It was a blessing to share our home, which had for so long been used in a wrong way, to promote friendship and unity.

On one occasion, I paid a visit to a home in the red-light district to see a member of the congregation, a renowned womaniser. He had the signs of the zodiac all round his room and was a bit of an unsavoury character. I knew his background and that he wanted a favour of me, although I didn't know what that might be. I felt strongly that visiting him amid such demonic surroundings was putting me at risk. He clearly had no intention of turning to God for help, and I told him that would be my one and only visit.

As I left his flat, I met Rosemary and we crossed the road on a zebra crossing. Rosemary was just in front of me and I was still on the crossing when I heard a terrific screech of brakes and a very loud bang. The car had hit a woman who had also been on the crossing, and had thrown her at least ten feet down the street. There was a large pool of blood, and people started crowding around her and calling the emergency services.

We realised we were lucky to be alive and, standing on the edge of the pavement as a large crowd had gathered, we thanked God for his protection and asked for his hand on her life. We never found out what happened to the woman, but given the severity of the accident I'm not confident that she could have survived it unless there was a miraculous intervention.

A visit from the bishop also proved problematic. While he oversaw the confirmations of two of our precious adult members and spent time ministering to and fellowshipping with us, we had some concerns over his attitudes and priorities. In fact, he caused me quite a number of problems during my time at Christ Church. I remember on one occasion when he got into my car telling him that he needed to fasten his seatbelt, which was quite true, but I chose my words rather mischievously and told him that he needed to "belt up". He didn't seem to catch the double meaning, but inwardly I felt mischievously gleeful!

Many years later it became common knowledge – affirmed by trustworthy media reports – that the bishop was alleged to have behaved very inappropriately some years earlier. This did not come as much of a surprise to me, and I presumed it was just the tip of the iceberg given my experience of him, but the moral failure of a man of authority within the Church is always particularly sad.

Even my personal health came under attack during the Easter of 1977. I returned to England as I was feeling unwell and spent five days in St Luke's Nursing Home for the Clergy in London. By the time I left, I had been given a clean bill of health, but I was sad to have missed our Easter celebrations at Christ Church.

Having said that, it was an absolute joy to spend a week with Rosemary, Giles and my parents in Guernsey as I recuperated, and we took many bracing walks along the magnificent coastal cliffs. There is nothing quite like family and mother nature to lift the spirits, and I gave all the glory to God for my swift recovery.

The highlights

Aside from the unpleasant underbelly and demonic oppression, Amsterdam was a fascinating city. The famous museums, including the famous Rijksmuseum, which houses Van Dyck paintings, were very interesting, as were the incredible art galleries. We also went to see Anne Frank's house, which was quite an experience. I found it difficult to put myself in her position and imagine the intense fear and distress of the situation, but the visit had a profound impact on us. We also enjoyed spending time in the fabulous parks and gardens the city had to offer.

Quite soon after we moved to Amsterdam, we returned to England for our dear Lin's wedding. It was a wonderful occasion and we so enjoyed spending time with family and friends while we were back. Her husband, Steve, is a committed Christian and has a great knack for languages. It was a great privilege to give her away, and to get to know Steve better.

A couple of months later we took a three-week holiday to Switzerland and had a lovely break in the mountains, leaving the Revd and Mrs Stevens from All Hallows Church, Twickenham, in charge while we were away. We returned feeling refreshed and strengthened in body, mind and spirit.

We welcomed a missionary named Elly van der Linden to a special harvest supper at the church, and she visited several times during our tenure in Amsterdam. She had come to know Jesus at Christ Church years earlier and was doing wonderful mission work in the Philippines. She showed some slides and spoke of her experiences as the only white woman on the island of Mindoro. It was very encouraging to hear what the Lord was doing in and through her.

On another occasion, we invited a group of young Christians from the *Logos* to the church to tell us about their life on board as volunteers, and about the wonderful work they were part of. Around fifty people attended the Ash Wednesday meeting to watch the film they put on and hear their great testimonies of faith. I was heartened to see that many of those in attendance generously gave to this great ministry and signed up to be prayer partners with some of the crew members, which I'm sure strengthened the faith of all involved.

Later on, we organised for a coachload of our Christ Church family to visit the ship in Rotterdam – about an hour from Amsterdam – which was a real eye-opener for those who came along. Frank Fortunato introduced us to the wonderful history of the ship and explained how Operation Mobilisation had grown over the years. The ship had docked in one hundred and twenty-five ports in forty countries over the previous five years. Almost two million people had visited the ship and another fifteen million had been presented with the gospel on shore.

A young woman named Alice Frost gave her testimony and then took the children to one side to tell them a bit more about Jesus. One of our congregation had taken her son Michael along, and he was deeply moved by what Alice said and by all the literature on board the ship. He received a long letter from her three days later and was so inspired by what she had written that, according to his mother, he sat down there and then and wrote a book!

My dear wife organised countless fundraising events, such as bring and buy sales, parish suppers and fashion shows, which helped us raise valuable funds for the church. As we had found in Ceylon, money was a constant struggle, albeit for different reasons. We knew that many members of the congregation could afford to give to the work of the church but actively chose not to, despite our best efforts to instil in them the biblical principles of giving.

Rosemary and the Ladies' Association helped to organise a Twelfth Night Supper, which attracted a large crowd. Along with delicious food, guests were treated to a talk from Rev Colin Bell of the English Reformed Church. He spoke of his invitation from the Queen to visit her for a weekend in Balmoral. Having initially thought it was a hoax, he had been picked up in one of the royal cars and enjoyed spending time with the Queen, Prince Philip and a host of other guests.

The Ladies' Association also arranged to sponsor a child in India; a seven-year-old girl named Sangita, who had just lost her mother and been placed in a children's home. This was, of course, an issue very close to Rosemary's heart having been born there and seen first hand the poverty in her birth nation.

I was constantly amazed and inspired by Rosemary's ingenuity in this area as she organised event after event. Of course, our chief aim in all that we did was to touch people's hearts and lives with the gospel, but we needed some additional funds to keep the Lord's work going. Over time, a growing number of church members began to give regularly, which helped us continue the work God had laid on our hearts.

Two of our young people, John and Claudette, travelled to England to get married. We invited them to an evening prayer meeting on their return to Amsterdam to tell us of the wonderful way in which the Lord had blessed, strengthened and upheld them after Claudette had learned of her mother's totally unexpected death the day before their wedding.

It was encouraging to hear how God had lifted them at such a time of sadness, just as they were about to begin a new chapter in their lives. Another member of the congregation who had attended the wedding testified of her strong sense of the Lord's presence on the day, which had made it a joyous occasion despite the family's tragic loss.

In addition to our Sunday school and youth meetings, we were blessed when Joop van der Elst, a regular member of the church with a wife and two babies, took it upon himself to teach some of the older children more about the Bible. God had placed the spiritual welfare of these older children on his heart and it was great to have someone step up in such a powerful way and instil in them important Christian principles that would equip them for life.

After the illness that had temporarily taken me back to the UK, I attended the National Evangelical Anglican Congress at Nottingham University with two thousand other participants. It had a deep and lasting impact on each of us, both through the teaching and the precious Christian fellowship. The theme was 'Obeying Christ in a Changing World', and it reminded me of the early Church and the incredible influence it had. We raised the roof in song, discussed new ways of proclaiming Jesus as Lord and had a great time just being together in an atmosphere of prayer and praise. What a blessing after all the difficult things we had been dealing with at Christ Church.

In the summer of 1977, Rosemary, Giles and I spent some glorious time camping in Switzerland, Austria and the north of Italy. We were drenched more or less the whole time due to the constant downpours, but it also made us realise what a blessing water is and why Jesus described himself as 'living water'. It's a powerful thing! We found the Furka Pass in Switzerland utterly breathtaking and awe-inspiring as the Rhone gushed down towards the Mediterranean.

We later stood in clouds of spray right beneath the Rhine where it plunges into the stupendous Rhinefall near Schaffhausen. Rivers of living water indeed! On turning from this tremendous spectacle, our eyes fell on the brass plaque on a nearby rock that read: "Let everything that hath breath praise the Lord. Praise ye the Lord." We did just that, and the still, small voice of the Lord spoke right into our hearts.

During the first week of this holiday, Lin and Steve stayed at the same hotel as us for three nights on their way home from a holiday in Prague. It was so lovely to catch up with them and to hear all their news. They had been praying faithfully for us throughout the tough times, which was greatly appreciated.

We also welcomed our Singaporean friend Keng from Christ Church during the last week of our holiday and enjoyed some exhilarating tobogganing high up in the mountains. We enjoyed the kind hospitality and warmth extended by the congregations of All Saints, Vevey, and St Peter's, Chateau D'Oex, where I ministered during our time away.

Healing hearts

Back in Amsterdam, I paid sixteen visits in two months to a man incarcerated in Huis Van Bewaring prison, which later became a hotel. This twenty-five-year-old Dutch prisoner was open to hearing the gospel, and I was able to share the wonderful message of God's love with him.

During this period, I witnessed a real miracle in his life, and this change was affirmed by his prison directors, chaplains, social workers and fellow prisoners. Having left home at the age of thirteen in search of his father, with blind hate in his heart and a knife in his hand, he suddenly decided to accept Jesus as his Lord and Saviour. I have no doubt that he shared this good news with his cellmate, a convicted murderer, and many others at the prison.

Long after we had left Amsterdam, while I was a chaplain in France, I received a personal letter from the choir mistress who had caused me so much trouble during my tenure there. She had eventually given her heart to the Lord, and she wrote the letter to apologise and ask me to forgive her for her behaviour. It just so happened that the next ICS meeting was in Amsterdam and she was present. Rosemary and I went right up and hugged her, and told her that we had long since forgiven her. I gathered subsequently that she wasn't completely free from the things of the past, but I was glad to see that God was moving in her life.

Words in season

There was a full church in December 1978 when Revd Richard Wurmbrand came to speak. An ever-faithful servant of God, he spoke both morning and evening, despite having pneumonia! We were all touched by what he said. In the morning, he spoke of examining ourselves. Having previously spent many years in solitary confinement, he had discovered that he no longer knew who he was. He felt as though he had become an imitation of others and had needed to examine his heart and rely on God to reaffirm his identity and transform his mind. It was a pertinent word and one that challenged us all.

In the evening he spoke about Nicodemus, who, despite his extensive education, had no idea what Jesus had meant when he said that Nicodemus needed to be born again if he wanted to see the kingdom of heaven. This had also come as a shock to me on that running track in Oxford, and I'm sure many who consider themselves to be good Christians know nothing of being born again.

It simply means that, through Jesus, we are spiritually born into God's family. Without being born again, we will always have something missing from our lives and will not be able to enjoy the richness of a close relationship with God, which is the very reason we're alive!

Richard's message was wholly consistent with what I had been preaching at the church myself, but sometimes it is easier for a guest speaker to preach a message than the minister, and I believe lives were changed as a result of our joint efforts.

Bishop Ambrose Weekes visited us in January 1979 and what a difference compared with our previous bishop's visit! The time he spent with us was largely unprogrammed and informal, so we felt that we were able to get to know him much better with no pomp and circumstance getting in the way. Virtually all members of our sixty-five-strong congregation attended a special supper and he made a great effort to speak to everyone and took a real interest in their lives. He was a truly humble and godly man.

For some reason, I found myself feeling quite down and despondent in March 1979, and it affected my ability to write sermons. At this very time, I was asked by two female students at the university to give an interview about the British sense of humour! They had been subjected to several blasphemous jokes during an interview with another British man in a pub, so they really seemed to appreciate an altogether different brand of humour.

We enjoyed a few good jokes and somehow, having offered up a silent prayer, God opened the way for me to tell them about his great love for them. It's amazing how, even when we feel low ourselves, the Lord not only lifts us, but uses us to lift others.

We could never complain that life was too quiet or dull in Amsterdam! Our time in the city may have been tumultuous at times, but we learnt a great deal and felt

God's presence in a very real way. While we came to realise the reality, power and personality of Satan in Amsterdam, we also discovered more of the greater power in the name of Jesus and the blood he shed for us.

This was the most rewarding and fulfilling time of ministry I had experienced up to this point, and without the tough times it would have been impossible to know God as intimately as I do now, or to handle the assignments that were to come. After almost five years in Amsterdam, the Lord was moving us on to our next adventure. Rosemary and I were off to France, while Giles attended boarding school back in Guernsey.

8. VIVE LA FRANCE!

"He said to them, 'Go into all the world and preach the gospel to all creation.'"

Mark 16:15

After a short spell back in the UK, Rosemary and I found ourselves away on our travels again, and this time our destination was France. I had served with ICS in Amsterdam, and an opening for a chaplain in Lyon and Grenoble – in the Rhône-Alpes chaplaincy – had come up. It was an area of such great natural beauty that our surroundings were a continual witness to the glory and majesty of God to all who visited the region. After the many ups and downs of our previous placement, we hoped that France would offer us a more sedate yet equally challenging opportunity. We weren't disappointed.

These days, Lyon and Grenoble are separate chaplaincies, but back then the chaplain was responsible for both cities, which were approximately eighty-five miles apart. My predecessor, a super chap for whom I had great respect, had decided that he would only go to Grenoble every other week.

This was perfectly understandable, but as the new chaplain I felt it would be a good idea to go every week as I didn't want the congregation in Grenoble to feel as though it were a poor relation of the Lyon parish. It also dispelled any confusion about which week the church service in Grenoble would take place.

This meant that we had a long drive between the morning and evening services each Sunday, but on the whole we didn't mind it. I took the morning service in Lyon and the evening service in Grenoble, and every other week we would stay over in Grenoble with kind members of the congregation and hold a Bible study on the Monday evening.

This really helped us get to know the members of both congregations, which were markedly different, and to serve them more effectively. Despite the distance between St Marc's in Grenoble and Mains Ouvertes (Open Hands) in Lyon, there was an atmosphere of great unity among our flock, and we praised God for that.

I remember one Christmas we had a lot of snow, and we were caught in a snow blizzard on our way to Grenoble. It was freezing cold and we were stranded, so I trudged off up the road to the nearest house to get help. I was up to my knees in snow! I had to phone the church wardens to let them know that we wouldn't be able to get there. Thankfully, they were able to take the service without me and we were able to get back to Lyon in one piece.

We lived in a comfortable house on a hill in southwest Lyon and thoroughly enjoyed the sizeable garden, which was right next to a large wood. We often saw squirrels popping out of the trees and in summer were kept awake by the numerous noisy nightingales! From the hills just above the house, it was possible to see the majestic peak of Mont Blanc on a clear day.

Being in the perfect location and with plenty of snow, I would have liked to ski regularly during our time in France. I only managed to go once while we were there, which was disappointing. I had been several times to Switzerland with my uncle as a youngster and enjoyed the sport very much. I had managed to pass the beginner's stage quite quickly and would have loved to build on my skills, but we were so busy with the ministry there was little time for recreation!

Reaching out

My primary ministry was to the approximately four thousand English-speaking people scattered about the region. Regular attendance was fairly low, with between twenty-five and forty joining us in Lyon and between twenty and thirty-five attending in Grenoble each week.

Most of our regular attendees were middle-aged, but we also had some young 'assistantes' (trainee British teachers attached to French schools), students and au pairs as well as a number of small children. Once quite a rarity in our parish, around twenty-five percent of our congregation was made up of babies and young children. Rosemary helped at the mums and babies group, which was a great way of supporting young families in the church and reaching out to others in the community.

Lyon had become quite a renowned business and scientific research hub, which brought plenty of young families our way. We experienced quite a rapid turnover as people came and went with their jobs, and it was always great to welcome new people in, albeit sad to see our friends leave for their next work assignments. These Christians who were temporarily with us for work were often able to witness to new contacts in their workplaces as well as through their varied social endeavours.

Our church secretary in Lyon, Karen May, was involved in a large English-speaking organisation for ladies in the city called The Monday Club, which gave her the opportunity to share her faith with a relatively large number of local women. Three members of our congregation were also interviewed about their faith on a radio programme, which was broadcast to a vast French audience. It was great to see the impact of these experiences on their own faith as well as in the lives of those around them.

We also welcomed many holidaymakers to take Communion with us. Some were regular churchgoers who were used to taking Communion in their churches back home, while others were new to it. However, all were welcome and it was great to be able to share some of God's heart with them even while they were away from their regular, day-to-day lives. Visitors always commented on the warmth and friendliness of our congregations, and many believers were delighted to find a little enclave of 'real Christians' in this remote setting.

Rosemary organised a number of buffet suppers at the vicarage, which served a dual purpose. They allowed us to get to know our congregation better and also enabled us to raise such much-needed funds for the Church Missionary Society. Our new friends thoroughly enjoyed these get-togethers, and despite some negative assumptions about British cuisine seemed to be very appreciative of Rosemary's cooking! After charging very little the first time round, we were urged to up the rate by those who came! It was a great way to fellowship beyond the formality of our church services.

Every week we held a prayer fellowship supper at the vicarage, which was attended by half a dozen or so young people. We had a time of worship – which was greatly improved when there was a guitar player among us – and prayer for around forty-five minutes before eating together and catching up. In the autumn and winter months we would stoke up a blazing log fire, which gave the vicarage a really cosy feel.

We weren't the only ones doing the hosting. Many families in our two churches welcomed us into their homes as a couple as well as holding dinners and barbecues for church members. One of our dear friends, Ann Clement, hosted a rice lunch on one occasion to raise money for refugees. She managed to raise five hundred francs for her cause and everyone enjoyed the lunch immensely.

Each year, we went on a parish weekend away to the marvellous Château de Chapeau Cornu. It was a wonderful time of 'recreation' in every sense of the word. Set in stunning countryside, we thoroughly enjoyed taking long walks as a church – with people joining us from both Lyon and Grenoble – and sharing meals together. It was a great way to recharge the batteries and build on friendships, and the Lord really blessed these times away. Giles had remained at school in Guernsey, and again we missed him terribly. He came to stay with us during his long holidays, which was always a delight.

Spiritual darkness

It may sound odd to some people, but France is quite a difficult country spiritually, or it certainly was at this time. People were generally very welcoming on a personal level, but there was a hardness there when it came to sharing the gospel. Many of those living around us were Catholic and did not share my belief that it was essential to be born again in order to become a real follower of God. This led to some difficult conversations, but God opened unexpected doors and gave me the right words to say on so many occasions.

I also discovered that Lyon was the headquarters in France for many satanic cults. Although we encountered dark forces there in a less direct way than in Amsterdam, the devil was clearly active in the city, as he is wherever he is given free rein.

I was greatly saddened to hear that a Russian lad in his fourth year at school in France had been battered to the point of losing consciousness because he was a Christian. While that was an extreme case, there was certainly resistance to the Christian faith from many quarters. It also saddened me to learn that there were more committed Christians per capita in the Soviet Union, where religion was banned, than in France (and, as an aside, the UK!).

We met a man named George Seyki from Ghana and discovered that he had spent some of his childhood living with his grandmother, who was an idol-worshipper. While even at a young age he found it strange that these idols were unable to do a great deal to help their worshipper when it came to getting a good education or having children, he had also been drawn into this darkness.

However, he had finally turned his back on idol worship, and a short time later he came to one of our open-air outreach events. He heard the verse, "Come unto me, all who have heavy loads, and I will give you rest" and decided that if God could help him, he might as well just accept Jesus Christ as his personal saviour!

Having seen the incredible difference prayer made in Amsterdam, I decided to devote a good deal of time to prayer while we were in France: on my own, with Rosemary and with members of the congregation. I officially made myself available every Tuesday at our Mains Ouvertes centre for those who wanted to come for a time of prayer, but our parishioners knew that they could call on me at more or less any time if they needed prayer support. We also held weekly Bible studies and enjoyed regular fellowship in people's homes.

Encouraging signs

It's never easy to quantify the impact of a ministry like this, but it was a wonderful highlight to see some of the people we came into contact with come to know the Lord in a real way. I remember one couple particularly as they had been through quite an experience before they gave their lives to Jesus.

While on honeymoon in Switzerland, they had returned to their hotel to find that an avalanche had basically flattened it. Had they been inside, they would surely have perished. While it didn't instantly make them reconsider their mortality or their need for God, they did eventually open their hearts to him, and they became great friends of ours.

We got to know another couple, Barry and Denise Shears, very well and I had the privilege of leading them to the Lord almost two years apart (read the full story, and two other testimonies in Appendix 2).

A French Catholic friend had suggested that they visit the 'English church' not long after they arrived, and they had diligently done so. Both had been baptised, confirmed and married in church, but were far from enjoying a living faith in Christ. They had been coming to the church for some time and hearing me preach, but it took a while for the word of God to sink in and change their hearts.

Denise was the first to realise that what she had accepted as Christianity bore no relation to the life of commitment and change I was preaching from the pulpit. She was pregnant at the time and, after what she described as a particularly moving sermon, she decided to make up her mind before the baby demanded too much of her time and attention. She asked me to really explain what it meant to be born again and I had the privilege of leading her to the Lord just three days before their son Daniel was born.

It took Barry a little longer to make a commitment, but I could tell over time that his heart was beginning to change, in no small part due to the newfound faith of his wife. They found it difficult to agree on anything during the time when they couldn't agree on this most important subject, and there were tensions between them as a result.

Thankfully, God intervened! Barry heard his Heavenly Father speaking to him and calling him into the kingdom, and he answered that call. As well as being wonderful parents and excellent friends, Barry and Denise had a real heart for elderly people and went on to run an old people's home in Crediton. I'm sure they are a great blessing to all the residents there.

Towards the end of our time in France, we befriended a dear man named Pierre Osiris, whom we initially found sleeping under a tree in Lyon. He was originally from Haiti and had been in hiding because he had the same name as a well-known terrorist and he firmly believed he was being hunted by the government. Our relationship grew over time and he began to call us Mum and Dad, which was very sweet. He was an intelligent young man, but had come from a very difficult background. We did what we could to help him financially and in prayer, and we are confident that he came to know the Lord personally.

Years after we had returned to the UK, I received a letter from a man named Duncan Powell. He had been with us in Lyon back in 1981 and had visited our home for lunch several times after the Sunday services and attended some of our Bible studies. Although we weren't incredibly close at the time, his letter was very moving.

He had attended a home group meeting and all the participants had been encouraged to make contact with someone who had played a significant part in their faith journey. After a period of quiet contemplation, my name came to Duncan's mind and he decided to write to me, thanking me for the spiritual direction and hospitality I had offered him.

I didn't remember doing anything particularly special, but I felt honoured that God had used me to help Duncan grow closer to his heavenly Father. I had felt that he was somewhat on the fringes of things at the time, but I was hugely encouraged to hear that he was really going on with the Lord. Now married, he has three children, all of whom have been brought up to know the truth of the gospel. He also told me that he had been very ill with a brain tumour, but that God had intervened in a miraculous way and he was on the road to recovery. Praise the Lord!

Once again, we felt God was calling us back to England, so we packed our bags, waved goodbye to our wonderful congregations and headed home. We felt sorry to be leaving so many great friends behind, but it was wonderful to be reunited with family and friends, not least Giles, who was twenty and at Leeds University by this time.

Our time in France was nowhere near as dramatic or rocky as Amsterdam, but we could see God's hand at work, gradually stirring people's hearts as we gave them the good news of Jesus Christ and invited them into our home for many wonderful times of fellowship.

9. A FINAL ADVENTURE

"Then I heard the voice of the Lord saying, 'Whom shall I send? And who will go for us?' And I said, 'Here am I. Send me!'"

Isaiah 6:8

We returned to England in 1985 and I experienced great difficulty in finding a new placement. I had served with the Intercontinental Church Society (ICS) in both the Netherlands and France, but I did not initially receive any funding from them on our return home.

I was constantly looking for opportunities and seeking God to find out where he would lead us next, but we had to wait a while before the future became clear. Having always been on the go, and reliant on the Lord to guide my steps, I'll admit that I struggled with my patience levels at times and felt rather frustrated not to immediately find fulfilling employment.

Temporary employment

Rosemary and I had kept on a flat in East Twickenham, so we returned there for a while. I spent some time working with a Roman Catholic priest in Tower Hamlets, down in the East End of London. I served with him at a homeless shelter, and going to and from work I often passed the pub where the Kray Brothers had famously gathered to plan their exploits. It wasn't the most salubrious neighbourhood, but I could see the great need there and was happy to help out on a temporary basis.

The people who came to the shelter were quite a rough bunch and we had to call the police fairly frequently. Alcohol and drugs were forbidden on the premises, but our guests managed to smuggle illicit substances in and trouble almost certainly followed.

I had to laugh on one occasion. We often served up food that was just past its sell-by date but still perfectly fine to eat, which had been donated by a big supermarket. One day I was dishing up Dover sole, and I remarked on it to one of our visitors, thinking he would be impressed by the calibre of food on offer.

"Oh, not Dover sole again!" he replied.

The phrase "Don't look a gift horse in the mouth" sprang to mind!

Following that brief assignment, Rosemary and I worked together for a short while at Tearfund in Teddington. I was on the assembly line packing food parcels, while Rosemary was at another workstation in the cavernous building. It was a wonderful organisation with a global reach, and we really appreciated the work the charity was doing.

One thing that impressed us very much was the devotion to prayer. A bell would ring mid-morning, and everyone would leave whatever they were doing and head into the meeting room for a time of prayer. It makes such a difference to be able to pray with like-minded people at work, a privilege so few have these days, and the atmosphere at Tearfund was rather special as a result.

A move up north

All the while, I was still looking out for longer-term roles and I kept in touch with various organisations, including the Church Pastoral Aid Society (CPAS) for news of upcoming vacancies. I heard there was an opening for a team vicar up in Stoke-on-Trent through CPAS and felt I should apply.

God opened the door for me and we moved to the diocese of Lichfield. It was strange to be back in ministry on British soil, but we enjoyed our time in Stoke and ended up staying there for almost six years before our next and final overseas adventure began.

Bagnall offered a small country church set in a close-knit community and, while people were very welcoming, it was a big change from our previous chaplaincies. I found that I had relatively free rein when it came to the church. When I arrived, the altar was right up against the east wall, and I felt it would be better for it to be shifted forward so that I could face the congregation as I stood behind it. Up until then, everyone had assumed that it couldn't be moved as it looked very heavy.

I said to the wardens, "Let's have a go," and when we did we found that it weighed little more than an ordinary table. Perhaps the most surprising part was that no one from the congregation made any comment at all about the new position.

The rector was in charge of four parishes, and the four team vicars, myself included, oversaw his own particular church. As I had been out of touch with normal parochial work in the UK, I was a bit unsure of some of the rules and regulations. The church needed a new carpet and I decided a red carpet would look nice, so I went ahead and bought it without getting permission from the diocese to make the purchase. It never occurred to me to do so. Such was the parish that no-one seemed to mind.

Soon after we arrived in Bagnall, I went to see the Bishop of Lichfield, a lovely man. This was standard practice to get to know one another's affairs. The bishop said to me, "I don't suppose you're related to AC Bradley, are you?" Andrew Cecil Bradley just happened to have been my great-uncle. He had been Britain's top Shakespearean scholar and his published work was highly acclaimed. The bishop had studied AC Bradley's works at university and gone on to become a professor of poetry at Oxford. It was another illustrious ancestor moment!

This time, however, I was able to hold my head up high. I hadn't reached the heady academic heights of my predecessors, but I knew that God had used me, and would continue to use me, to build his kingdom. I had finally come to realise that there was no greater calling than that.

On one occasion, I remember a lady coming to the front of the church for prayer. She had terrible arthritis in her hands, to the point where she could barely move them. They looked more like claws than hands. I remember holding her hands in mine and praying over her. God touched her miraculously, and her hands straightened out. They became functional again and the pain disappeared. It was a powerful reminder of the Lord's healing power and ability to make all things new.

I soon realised that many people came into contact with the church for various reasons, for example to lay flowers on gravestones or to ring the bells, but the majority didn't attend the services. It was rather sad to see people get so close and then back off before they could get involved. Rosemary and I made a great effort to build relationships with members of the local community, but there was a clear lack of enthusiasm about matters of faith.

Despite our long tenure in Bagnall, we only saw a few come to a real Christian faith. Nevertheless, every lost sheep is incredibly precious to God, and it was a privilege to help lead these people to Christ. Being so remote, we felt it was a bit of a testing time, especially as people in the area seemed to have very fixed ideas about things. However, times of testing are always valuable as they prepare us for the next adventure God has for us!

Exploring the Emirates

The next adventure just so happened to be in Dubai and Sharjah. In our heart of hearts, Rosemary and I had been hoping for one last stint abroad before I retired, and we had started seeking God for an opportunity.

A minister I knew called Dennis Gurney had placed an advert in his church magazine looking for someone who was ordained, but nearing the end of his ministry, to serve alongside him as associate chaplain. God had obviously heard our prayers! He was looking for an assistant to be in charge of the chaplaincy in Sharjah, while he continued to oversee the work in Dubai, where he had been based for around ten years. Various answers to prayer later, we felt that this was God's will and the next thing we knew, our bags were packed and we were off once again!

Lin, Jane and Giles were all very grown up by this point, of course. Giles had attended Leeds University, initially studying Economics before changing his course to Theology. He then moved to Salisbury and then Southampton while continuing to work for a life insurance company in Salisbury. Lin and Steve were living in Birmingham, while Jane and Tim were in Oxford, and we had four grandchildren by this time! It was great to see our three children progressing in their careers, families and faith. We missed them as always, but they all came out to visit us while we were in the UAE, so that was a great blessing.

I had first met Denis decades before when I had preached at his church in Jersey on behalf of the ICS following our time in Ceylon. While we were in Lyon and Grenoble, he kindly filled in for me while we were on holiday in Guernsey. He stayed at our house in Lyon for two or three weeks and did a great job of preaching and handling parish matters in our absence.

Our meetings with him up to this point had been fairly brief, but we knew God was ordering our steps and I looked forward to knowing him better. It turned out he was a man of enormous energy! One almost had to trot to keep up with him at walking pace. It was instantly apparent that he was doing a remarkable work in Dubai and we met up regularly to pray together as the congregations were only around twenty-two miles apart.

We each had chaplaincy cars, but while Rosemary and I were on home leave in Guernsey, Denis had borrowed mine while his was at the garage. He kindly came to pick us up in his own car, which had been repaired by this point. He was full of apologies as he confessed that he had been driving our car at quite a pace and had hit a camel. He had somehow had the sense to swerve to his right, but the camel had hit the front of the car and completely crushed it. He was lucky to have survived, which was more than could be said for the car!

While I was in Dubai, I went along to the blood bank to check whether my blood was suitable for use in transfusions. Despite my having served in the Tanganyikan police, I was sickened at the sight of flowing blood, which caused me to avert my gaze immediately. I knew that my trembling knees could easily pitch me forward in a dead faint. However, I was determined to give blood because the health service always desperately needed donations, although the thought of it filled me with horror.

The nurse had just jabbed the needle into my arm when I promptly passed out! I ended up lying on the floor. When I came round, the British nurse was as white as a sheet and frantically trying to resuscitate me. It was most embarrassing! Thankfully, my aversion to needles is no longer a problem, which I believe to be a deliverance from God in light of what was soon to come.

Shepherding a friendly flock

I had great difficulty writing my first sermon, which was on the subject of Nicodemus, from John 3. The din from the some of the mosques all around was so colossal that it was almost impossible to think. We couldn't fault the locals on their dedication, but the regular calls to prayer were a major distraction. Nevertheless, I finally managed to get it written and the congregation seemed very receptive.

We had a handful of Brits at St Martin's – which was actually based at an RAF building rather than in a proper church building – but the majority were of Indian, Sri Lankan and Filipino origin. This was a welcome development as far as we were concerned, as we had such a great love for India from our travels, and for Sri Lanka following our time in Colombo. Having both been born in Asia, we felt a real kinship with our little flock of around thirty to thirty-five people.

During the three years we were in Sharjah, we made some wonderful friends and felt we were really able to encourage our small congregation in their faith. Most were economic migrants, working hard to support their struggling families back home, although a few were extremely affluent, having taken full advantage of the burgeoning economy. The God of Mammon is certainly in evidence in Dubai! It's a fabulous place, but it's all money, money, money, and we felt there was a great spiritual need in the region.

Life in the Emirates was more uncertain than in many parts of the world due to the issues arising around visas, work situations and nationality issues. We were constantly reminded that we were guests in the region, and we never knew who would be the next to leave due to a visa refusal or a work contract termination. This created a certain level of tension, but fortunately we were able to trust our heavenly Father to meet our needs and guide our steps. While this didn't always change people's circumstances, it helped to give us peace that God was in control whatever happened.

The majority of our parishioners were from church backgrounds, so our role was to teach the congregation how to be more like Jesus rather than facilitating dozens of conversions, although we did see one or two people give their hearts to the Lord while we were in Sharjah.

Despite being a Muslim country, there were no restrictions on church meetings or on what we were at liberty to say. That might have been a different story had we taken to the streets proclaiming Jesus, but as I was largely preaching to believers, we were left very much to our own devices by the authorities and we didn't feel any risk in our being there.

On one occasion, we attended a gathering in a large arena in Dubai. We estimated that there were around a thousand people there. As we worshipped the Lord, people began speaking and singing in tongues. Early on in my faith, I had been somewhat suspicious of the gift of tongues, but when I received it I soon realised that it was a huge blessing, and it revolutionised my prayer life. It was an incredible experience to be there in the midst of it, united in our passion and overflowing in the Holy Spirit. If you ever have the chance to attend such a gathering, grasp it with both hands!

Wonderful testimonies

Every few weeks, part of my job was to go to Fujairah, so I had to drive across the desert, which was quite fun. One of the most remarkable Christians we ever met lived in Fujairah. His name was Tom and his wife was Edna. Tom had a ministry to Muslims in Saudi Arabia and many other countries in the Middle East where it's illegal to speak about Christianity.

He was extremely bold and would purposefully use transparent bags to transport Bibles and Christian literature to places where they were banned. Over the years, the Lord has opened doors for him in extraordinary ways and it was amazing to hear his many testimonies.

I was interested to hear that he came from a very difficult background. His father had been an alcoholic and used to beat his mother, and all the children had been very afraid of him. The family was so poor that they couldn't afford to buy shoes. Yet despite his humble and traumatic start in life, God used Tom powerfully to witness of his great love and mercy to people who might never have heard such a message before.

On one occasion, Tom had a dramatic fall from a ladder while he was taking a look at a water tank twenty feet up from the cement ground. The ladder slipped and he fell, but the Lord miraculously turned him around in midair so that he landed on his back, or he would no doubt have been killed. Fortunately, his hands were in front of his face, which protected his skull, but his arms were completely fractured. It was a miracle that he survived.

We made friends with a lovely Indian couple while we were in Sharjah. The husband had an important job at the cement factory and, like Tom, suffered a very nasty accident. He fell and hurt his leg very badly, to the point where the experts weren't sure that it would ever function properly again. I prayed over his leg several times, and while there wasn't an instant healing, it vastly improved over time and he was soon able to walk again.

Many labourers in this region had fallen to their deaths or been severely injured at work. The health and safety laws were lax, and there seemed to be little concern for the welfare of the primarily migrant workforce. Those who were disabled rather than killed were simply kept out of sight, as disability wasn't acceptable in society at that time. Dubai was the playground of the rich and famous, but it was a difficult place for the many imported workers, who had very few rights or privileges.

We also got to know a family from Nigeria well. They were committed Christians and really vocal about their faith, which was a joy to see. One day I received a phone call from the father, Joe, who was clearly distraught. They had been down at the beach together as a family and one of the boys had been drowned. Another of their sons had been saved at the last moment. We were shattered to hear the news and did all we could to offer comfort to the family at this terrible time.

Joe was convinced that God would raise his son from the dead. I accompanied him to the crematorium, where he proceeded to lay hands on the boy's body and pray loudly for him to be brought back to life. I also prayed for father and son, and was able to reassure Joe that he could look forward to the day when they would meet again in heaven. He never stopped praising the Lord, even in this saddest of circumstances.

I had the privilege of speaking at the son's funeral and was amazed at how strong the family remained in their faith, continuing to thank God for his goodness throughout. They eventually moved to Canada, where Joe took up leadership of a church. No doubt this tragic experience gave him the ability to support others undergoing terrible trials, as well as encouraging them in their faith through his own dedication to the Lord.

We made friends with another couple in Sharjah. The wife was much more committed in her faith than the husband, and she and Rosemary grew quite close. The husband had a very good job and they had a fantastic home in Sharjah as well as a stunning property back home in Southern India. They kindly insisted on almost entirely financing a trip to India so that we could take a holiday. The husband even provided a chauffeur-driven car, which was very kind, although we found it a little embarrassing being driven around in the lap of luxury while there was such abject poverty all around us.

Lively fellowship

As always, Rosemary was a truly wonderful wife and an invaluable help to me. She helped with the women's work at the church and, as always, offered fantastic hospitality when people came back to our home. Former Archbishop of Canterbury, Lord Robert Runcie, came to visit on one occasion and we had the pleasure of entertaining him at our house.

The congregation was very excited that an archbishop from England had travelled all that way. Our sitting room was even more packed than usual, and we had great fun. One of our livelier girls, Sheba, told us jokingly that she was determined to give him a kiss on his cheek. It rather surprised us when she followed through with her promise! It was a delight to have him with us, and to hear him preach here and there, while he was in the region.

Various fundraising initiatives took place while we were in Sharjah, including a sponsored swim, bottle collections, choir celebrations and a charity ball. As with every other posting, it was essential to maintain a steady stream of income in order to carry out the mission. It was great to see everyone getting involved and supporting these activities, which often provided a source of fun as well as a much-needed financial boost.

Operation Mobilisation visited Dubai twice during our three-year stay, this time in the form of its second ship, the *Doulos*. We met George and Drena Verwer again on both occasions, which was a real treat. I also invited a group from the ship to speak at the church in Sharjah, and each member had an interesting testimony to share.

One girl had been at a church in South Africa when a massacre occurred. Terrorists had attacked the church in Cape Town in 1993, killing eleven people and injuring fifty-five. This girl had managed to hide as best she could on the floor while a man with a machine gun circled the area looking for more victims.

She somehow survived the attack and her testimony was extremely moving. Despite the deeply traumatic event, she clearly had unwavering faith in God and had devoted her life to sharing the gospel with others. It was an amazing example of how the Lord is able to turn even the worst experiences to good for those who love him (see Romans 8:28).

More goodbyes

After three years in Sharjah, it was time to 'retire'. I celebrated my sixty-fifth birthday there in 1997, and we made preparations to return to Guernsey. We had long since bought a family home there for our retirement and, while we returned with heavy hearts, it was a joy to have a lovely house and all our family and friends to come back to. While we knew this was to be our last overseas adventure, we were confident that God wasn't retiring us completely. After all, there's no such thing as retirement from the Lord's work!

Everyone at St Martin's clubbed together and put together a fantastic banquet to bid us farewell, in addition to sending us away with a generous financial gift. We were very touched by their kindness, which had been evident throughout our stay. Hospitality had always been at the heart of our ministry, and our congregation had reciprocated with incredible warmth and generosity.

10. LATER LIFE

"My flesh and my heart may fail, but God is the strength of my heart and my portion forever"
Psalm 73:26

We were warmly welcomed back to Guernsey and enjoyed catching up with friends and family. Having moved around so much, it was difficult to say where we really came from this side of heaven, but we still had strong links with the island and were active members of Holy Trinity church.

Years earlier, I had preached at the church and, departing from my notes, had allowed the Holy Spirit to take over. It was a gospel message and I remember saying: "Even as I look at my darling wife, who's smiling up at me now, I can honestly say that I actually love Jesus Christ more than I love her."

Some people are surprised when you make statements like this, because in the world we should never admit to loving anyone more than our spouse or children! But Rosemary perfectly understood and continued to smile, and I think it really made some of the congregation reconsider about their own fervour for the Lord.

While we were still in Guernsey, we were asked by one of the largest local churches whether we could put someone up for the weekend. The man was Lord McColl, and it transpired that he was one of the leading lights of Mercy Ships, a wonderful organisation that voyages around the world to meet the medical, emotional and spiritual needs of people in some of the poorest countries.

We readily agreed to this and were privileged to hear about some of Lord McColl's experiences as one of the senior surgeons on board the ship. He had given up several years of his life to travel around performing life-changing operations. What an incredible ministry.

In 2005, we were delighted to hear that Giles had proposed to Sarah, and the couple were married in the December. The service was held in Tatworth, and the reception at Forde Abbey in Chard. I had the great privilege of taking the wedding and we were delighted to officially welcome Sarah into the family.

Falling ill

We settled comfortably back into life in the UK, moving from Guernsey to Exeter and then Exmouth. Rosemary and I got involved in prison ministry and were also active members of Holy Trinity Church in Littleham. However, we were about to discover that a time of great sadness was to follow. In 2010, my darling Rosemary was diagnosed with terminal ovarian cancer. We had enjoyed such a long and happy marriage, and it came as a great shock to us both that her life was drawing to an end.

As I was no longer working in any official capacity, I had the honour and privilege of caring for my dear wife during her long illness. Jane was a great help during this difficult time as she was a nurse and her husband Tim was in charge of the pain clinic at Churchill Hospital. Jane was able to ensure that her mother was a comfortable as possible towards the end. Lin and Giles were also a great support to us both as we came to terms with Rosemary's impending passing.

I did everything I could for Rosemary during her time of sickness, but on one occasion in 2006 I took a short break from caring for her to stay with Caroline in Harrogate. The physical and emotional impact of caring for my lovely wife had taken quite a toll and I needed to recharge my batteries so that I could continue to look after her well.

It was during my stay with Caroline that further trouble struck. The day before I was due to travel home, I began to feel that something wasn't quite right. I was knocking into things and clumsily mishandled the milk jug at the breakfast table.

Both Caroline and I realised that I had suffered a mini stroke, known as a transient ischaemic attack (TIA). My flight home was pre-booked, so I stuck with it, which probably would have gone against the advice of my doctor had he known! I then had the unpleasant task of breaking the news to Rosemary, who was suffering greatly herself.

Getting older is something we all have to deal with, and ill health is often a factor in our latter days, but we had never faced serious health issues before and we knew that we needed to keep God at the centre, even in the midst of our suffering.

Our local church was a great support and we relished the opportunity to have fellowship with real believers, which allowed us to speak openly and pray together regularly.

A major operation

I was very concerned about my declining health, not least because I wanted to be able to continue to care well for Rosemary. Months after the mini stroke, I was booked in for a carotid endarterectomy, an emergency operation to unblock one of my carotid arteries. The carotid arteries are the main blood vessels that supply the head and neck, so it was a major operation, and an urgent one, as blocked carotid arteries are often a precursor to TIAs and strokes. Had I had a further TIA or a full stroke, my speech and movement might have been permanently affected and I could even have lost my life. As it was, I had become terribly forgetful and confused about things I hadn't been before.

It wasn't until fairly recently that I realised this operation probably saved my life, but I was extremely impressed at the time by the way it was carried out. The five-and-a-half-hour operation took place under local anaesthetic, so I was awake the whole time. As I lay there, allowing the medical professionals to do their difficult jobs, I simply praised the Lord for his goodness and prayed silently in tongues. The medical team around me were chatting away and I just thought, "This is amazing."

They asked me to move my neck to the left and right every so often, and the nurse told me to squeeze his hand every ten seconds to make that sure I was still alive! At one point, the consultant had to be very diplomatic with his words. He didn't actually say, "Please keep still because I'm about to cut your throat," but that was, in fact, what was happening. By the grace of God, I had long since got over my fear of blood, or I would have been in all sorts of trouble!

Rosemary and Lin came to see me at the hospital the next day, and by then I was fully with it. I looked pretty bright and cheerful, and I started telling them about a conversation I had had with another man on the ward. This chap and I had got chatting and the opportunity had arisen for me to tell him about the Lord's incredible goodness to me over the years and to give him a tract I had with me.

I'm not sure what impact this had on the man, who was also in for a serious operation, but Rosemary and Lin appeared a little annoyed by my focus. "We've come to find out how you are!" they exclaimed. Once a minister, always a minister!

Saying goodbye

I returned home, and we spent several more happy years together – ill health aside – in our new home in Littleham, near Exmouth. Rosemary bore her sickness as well as she could and we played tennis almost up until the time of her death. My darling wife died peacefully at home on May 19, 2011, which was without doubt the saddest day of my life.

Although I had known it was coming for some years, it did nothing to soften the blow of her passing. We were married for nearly fifty years, and I think in all that time we were only separated for a week or two. Those years were filled with such incredible blessing and I am so deeply thankful that the Lord showed me the person I was supposed to marry. We had a wonderful marriage; it was an absolute blessing. I knocked about the world so much with Rosemary.

Rosemary's funeral was a very difficult occasion for the family. Despite having presided over hundreds of funerals during my time as a minister, nothing could have prepared me for the great sadness of losing my precious wife and dearest friend. The only consolation was knowing that the Lord had welcomed her into her eternal rest with open arms.

Caroline, Jane and Giles gave readings during the service, and Giles also gave an address after I had said a few words. He concluded by saying:

> *We will all miss you so much dear Mum, Granny, Rosemary, but I will end on a note of great hope by paraphrasing words of the well-known song:*
>
> *We'll meet again*
> *Don't know when*
> *But I do know where*
> *Yes I know we'll meet again*
> *Some happy day*

I miss her every day, and I know that the whole family and our many friends also suffered a great loss. Our children were a great blessing at the funeral, and then in the aftermath of sorting through Rosemary's things, making the many heartbreaking decisions that needed to be made during this time of intense grief. I was also heartened by the many cards of condolence we received from around the world. Rosemary had left her mark on so many people's lives.

Gracey Court

After Rosemary's death, I decided to sell our home and move into a residential home. My health still presented certain challenges and I felt the need for company having suddenly found myself without my closest companion. I decided on Gracey Court in Broadclyst, a home for retired Church of England clergy. By happy coincidence, it was just a stone's throw from the home of Giles and Sarah, and their dear children, Samuel and Anna.

It was such a comfort to know that I would finally be living close to my son after many years of painful separation while Rosemary and I were overseas, and that I could finally get to know him and his family better. Giles has so many gifts I always wished I had possessed. He can do anything of a technical kind and has been a great help to me over the years. Sarah and the children are an absolute delight, and I love spending time with them as a family.

Gracey Court, affectionately nicknamed 'Crazy Court', is a very interesting place to live and was quite a shift for me. Inhabited by a number of couples and some clergy who, like me, have lost their spouses, I soon found that a keen sense of humour was needed to settle in and enjoy this new life chapter. I have made some great friends at Gracey Court, and the staff are absolutely fantastic, but nothing could fill the chasm in my life that the departure of my darling wife had left. Interestingly, Gracey Court opened on May 19, 1993; exactly eighteen years before Rosemary died.

I don't know how those without faith deal with such a separation, but I am convinced that I would have fallen apart had it not been for God's continued goodness to me. One of the benefits of being at the home is that there is plenty of time for quiet reflection and prayer. Praying in tongues has been a special blessing, enabling me to press in to God even at times when I had no words to express how I was feeling.

If you don't have the gift of tongues, I would strongly recommend that you ask someone who does to pray with you to receive it, or to petition the Lord yourself. You'll be surprised at how it strengthens your faith in the good times and the bad. God knows what you're saying even if you don't, and many miracles have taken place as a result of people speaking in tongues.

During our years of ministry, we had been surrounded by people from all backgrounds and cultures, and I will admit that I have struggled at times with a sense of loneliness in this place of peaceful solitude. Gone are the days of having a full house of people laughing and praying together, with Rosemary always on hand to welcome people and provide delicious refreshments for all who came through the door.

Still, I thank God for his continued goodness and enjoy all the fellowship I can with those around me. One thing I still love to do is watch the many birds that land on my balcony and in the garden below. I miss pointing the different species out to Rosemary, who shared my love for birds, but seeing them reminds me how much God cares even for these beautiful creatures, and so much more for me.

Never a spare part

Sometimes when we get older we can feel as though we have outlived our usefulness, and the thought of being a burden on others can become a real fear. However, I have an unshakable confidence in my heavenly Father, who I know has more for me to do on earth before I go to be with him forever.

I share the leadership of a Bible study at Gracey Court and occasionally minister in the onsite chapel. I am also a member of the local church and, while it's quite different from the church Rosemary and I attended in Exmouth, I enjoy worshipping there alongside some fantastic Christians.

Beyond home and church life, I have had various opportunities to share the gospel with people I have come into contact with while out and about. On one occasion, I was able to share my journey of faith with a local hairdresser in her tiny shop. I could tell that she was listening carefully, as were the others in the shop. Unfortunately, she relocated shortly afterwards so I was unable to follow up, but I was glad I had taken the opportunity while it was there. Thankfully, when we sow the seeds, we can be sure that God will do the watering. I look forward to seeing her in heaven some day!

Another time I was travelling by train – where so many of my most influential conversations have taken place – and found myself talking to the lady sitting next to me. I have learnt over the years that it's important not to barge in with the gospel, but it was a five-hour journey, so I had plenty of time to strike up a decent conversation before naturally discussing matters of faith.

She seemed interested in the fact that I had travelled extensively, and I was able to share my Jonah-like experience with her. Shortly before I disembarked in Harrogate, I realised that it had been exactly sixty years to the day that I had met Eric James, who had inadvertently set me back on the road to recovery.

Looking back on my life, it's amazing to see how God has worked in and through me, even before I came to know Jesus as my Lord and Saviour. It never ceases to amaze me that God chose me to be his child and to share the hope I have in him with so many around the world. I want to honour the Lord for the people he has brought across my path in such an astonishing way, and for being so patient with me even when I was determined to run away! Even a total failure in the eyes of the world can be used to build the kingdom of God in some way.

While I have certainly done some things I regret over the years, I know that the past is forgiven and washed clean by the blood of Jesus, who died so that we might live. While some fear death, I'm so glad to have the assurance that when that day comes I'll go straight to my heavenly Father, who has prepared a special place for me (see John 14:1-4).

APPENDIX 1
KEY EVENTS IN MY LIFE

1932: Born in Hong Kong (my father was in the colonial service).

1934-36: Guernsey with my maternal grandparents (my parents were in Uganda).

1936-38: Uganda with my parents and my younger brother, Jeremy (my older sister Patty remained in Guernsey).

1938-40: Guernsey with my grandparents (Patty, Jeremy and I were evacuated on the last mail boat to England before the Germans arrived).

1940-45: Buxton as a refugee (briefly), then Henley-on-Thames with Ginny and Gabey (along with Jeremy).

1946-50: Lancing College.

1952-52: Oxford University (where I was saved).

1953-56: Training for and serving in Tanganyika (now Tanzania) as a police cadet superintendent.

1956-57: Sussex with Patty and her husband John (where I taught Latin for a term).

1957-58: Vancouver, Canada (doing odd jobs and unsuccessfully applying for the RCAF).

1958-62: London School of Divinity (subsequently ordained at St Paul's Cathedral).

1962-65: First curacy at Stephen's Church, East Twickenham (I married my lovely wife Rosemary in 1964).

1965-69: Second curacy at Christ Church, Herne Bay (our son Giles was born in 1965).

1969-71: Wilton, Teesside, with The Missions to Seamen.

1971-74: Colombo, Ceylon (now Sri Lanka) with The Missions to Seamen.

1974: Gravesend for six months, assisting at a local church with The Missions to Seamen.

1975-79: Christ Church Amsterdam as Anglican chaplain.

1979-85: Lyon and Grenoble, France, as an ICS chaplain.

1985-86: Twickenham working for Tearfund (where Rosemary also worked) and Tower Hamlets working for a homeless project with a Roman Catholic priest.

1987-93: Bagnall, Stoke-on-Trent as team vicar.

1993-97: St Martin's Sharjah, UAE, as associate chaplain.

APPENDIX 2
THREE SPECIAL TESTIMONIES

Keith and Caroline ("Cag") Wilson

Cag met Brian and Rosemary in Grenoble while living abroad for a year as part of her university course. Accepting a friend's invitation to attend the Bradleys' church, she was struck by Brian's powerful presentation of the gospel. She realised pretty early on that she would have to break up with Keith, her non-Christian boyfriend, which came as quite a surprise to him!

Cag: From the minute I stepped onto French soil, I came into contact with people who talked about Jesus. It was incredible. God was after me from the start! One was a chap called Tim, who went to Brian and Rosemary's church. He had a really evangelistic heart and had been praying for me, I think. All he talked about was Jesus, and I pricked my ears up at this. Eventually, after about six weeks, I thought, 'I'd like to go to that church,' and then he invited me.

The church in Grenoble had around 20 regular attendees at the time, and Cag instantly felt welcomed in and drawn to the gospel.

Cag: They were essentially doing services for English-speaking people living abroad. I went to my first service one evening, and basically heard the gospel for the first time, even though my background was one of dipping in and out of church. I'd been baptised and then confirmed as a youngster, but, looking back, I realise I'd been persuaded into confirmation due to peer pressure (I'd fallen away). I'd had a pretty negative experience really of church up until that point. I'd literally walked out on my confirmation day vowing I would never look into it again, because it was a load of rubbish as far I was concerned.

The first thing I heard Brian say was, "Did you know that Jesus loves you this much" – he held his arms open wide, as if it were a cross – "and died for you?" I'd probably heard it before, but I hadn't been ripe for hearing it, and that was the moment. It just really struck a chord with me.

I was blown away by the attitude of the people who were attending that service. They were just full of joy and smiling, and really loving to each other. That left a massive impression on me. I remember saying to Brian that night, "I don't know what they're eating or drinking, but I'd like some of that, please, and I'm not leaving until I get it." So that was the beginning of a lifelong friendship.

Back in the UK, Keith had finished university and was working for an accountancy firm in London. He didn't know it when he applied, but it turned out to be a Christian firm ("That's the Lord for you!" says Cag). He had even less of an idea that Cag was about to drop an unexpected bombshell on him.

Cag: We'd been going out less than a year at that point, and as soon as I went along to that church, and as soon I realised there was a choice to be made, I knew I had to write to Keith to tell him it was over. It was really harsh, but I needed space to concentrate on the Lord. We were non-Christians and we were sleeping together. It was really weird, because I wasn't even a Christian yet, but I thought, 'Well I can't be doing that on the one hand and then say I'm looking into the truth.'

I could see that the Lord was after me, and cornering me in every possible way, so I just wrote to Keith and I said, "Look, I've got to sort this thing out with God. I can't be sleeping with you and doing all that stuff, so let's call it a day for now. I think we just need to have some time."

It was at this point that Caroline's faith – and her deep friendship with Brian and Rosemary – really began to blossom.

Cag: Brian and Rosemary were amazing. They invited me back to their home in Lyon so many times. I remember it was February 10 and I was staying overnight. They'd put me up in their study. They had shelves and shelves of books. I absolutely hated reading – that was the bizarre thing – but I just devoured these books all night. I just sat up on my camp bed and read and read. I was so hungry for truth. One particular book was *Chasing the Dragon* by Jackie Pullinger. I read that, and I just thought, 'Wow, this God seems to be really real.' One morning, I couldn't resist God's call any longer, and with Brian as a witness I knelt on the study floor and gave my life to the Lord.

They were an amazing couple. They were just so hospitable. They always had people round, and always had people staying, or to lunch. They had an amazing ministry out there.

But there was more to come in the Cag and Keith's story. They had been broken up, and barely in touch, for almost three years when, Keith rang the family home out of the blue.

Cag: Keith was going to a work event at the Windsor Polo Club, where Prince Charles was going to be, and he said he needed to take someone with decent table manners! That was hysterical!

I went, but only to tell him the gospel. When I split up with him, I'd said, "Look, I'm sorry, but God is after me, and I need to find out if God is the truth. There's no other reason." I felt I owed it to him to go back and say, "The God I left you for is still the most important person in my life." We met, talked a lot, and I gave him a Bible. He went away in the summer on a lads' holiday and snuck the Bible into the toilet every morning to read John's Gospel. He became a Christian within thirteen weeks of us meeting again!

I really wasn't looking for a boyfriend, and I knew Keith wasn't a believer so didn't want to give him the wrong impression. But I prayed that, if this was the one God had for me, he would give his life to the Lord by his birthday, which was a terrible fleece to put out!

So I went to visit him on his birthday weekend, and I walked upstairs, and I just said, "Well, where are you at? You've heard the gospel, you know what's what. Are you in or out?" It was really amazing, because I never do things like that, but it just came out of my mouth.

He said, "Well actually, it's interesting that you should say that, because last Wednesday I went to the church, sought out the minister and gave my life to Jesus." I was like, "Oh my word. That means we're going to get married!" I knew from that moment. We got married about a year later, and he's been in the ministry for about twenty-two years now.

The couple have four children and are now settled back in Ashford following a five-year stint in the US. No matter how many years have passed since those early days of faith in France, Cag has never forgotten the impact Brian and Rosemary had on her then, or on her family later on.

Cag: I am eternally grateful for Brian! He's just the most amazing friend. Two of our children, Jesse and Abbey, went to Exeter University, so that was fantastic because it meant we could occasionally pop in on Brian and Rosemary. Brian also came to speak at one of our missions we did a few years ago. You could never meet anyone more full of Jesus than Brian. We just love him to bits.

I really feel that Brian and Rosemary were my spiritual parents because I don't think there's another Christian in our family, apart from our own kids, for generations. We really looked to Brian and Rosemary for all sorts of wisdom and prayers. I think Brian has prayed for us every Tuesday since I became a Christian. That's the sort of man he is. He's a very dear friend to us, and Rosemary was too. I've never met another couple like them.

Barry and Denise Shears

Barry and Denise Shears moved to Lyon in 1980, where Barry was working for a French multinational company. Though both had some experience of Christianity and Sunday school growing up, the couple weren't pursuing their faith in any meaningful way. Little did they know that their world was about to be turned upside down.

Denise: A Catholic lady who worked in Barry's office obviously thought that we needed God in our lives, and probably thought that we weren't speaking French very well, so it was no good sending us to a French church. She had a friend who went to Brian's congregation, so she kept pestering us to go along. In the end, we gave in. She'd even drawn us a map of how to get to the church, which was in the ecumenical centre in Lyon.

Barry: Between skiing and going to the beach and everything else, we sort of said, "All right, we'll go." It was wonderful, it really was. It was so inspiring from the word go. We got to know Brian and Rosemary well, joined Bible study classes and spent a lot of time with them and other members of the community there.

Denise: I was quite bowled over by Brian's preaching, right from the beginning. It was very direct. I wasn't working at the time as we'd decided that when we went to France we would start a family. I didn't speak French all that well – I learnt it in the end, but it took a while – so I had all the time in the world to explore Christianity. Brian lent me lots of books and we had frequent talks.

Barry: It was his integrity; his firm faith that impacted us. He just exuded a tremendous love for Christ. I think that's what attracted us to him. He was very evangelical. It was an all-age ministry and they had lots of students. Rosemary was always feeding them! Lyon was quite a spiritual desert. Rosemary related so well to everybody, and really was Brian's 'right-hand man'.

I seem to remember that when he first went along there as a minister, he found people using the church as a social club, so he started to preach the gospel, and a lot of people who were using it to arrange the next cocktail party couldn't stand it and left. We joined when things were a bit of a struggle, but he started to build it up again with his real evangelical message, which appealed to a lot of people.

He was running two churches at the time. So they would be at the Lyon church, and then they quickly had to pack their bags and drive off to Grenoble. We had joint visits and services and outings. There was quite a distance between the two, but a few times a year we'd get together.

Denise: The other thing was that he and Rosemary were so hospitable. We were pretty new to living in Lyon; we'd probably been there about three months then. The first thing they did was ask us over for a meal. This was outside my experience of vicars, I have to say. We got to know them as friends, and we carried on going to the church.

It took about eighteen months for the penny to drop with me. I think I was also waiting for Barry to come to that point, which for him came a bit later on. I was pregnant by that time, and our first baby was a little bit late in arriving, and I felt, 'I've got to make up my mind before the birth of the baby.' So basically, that's what I did. It was after a particular Sunday message.

I remember phoning Brian and Rosemary on the Monday and saying, "I want to become a Christian. How do I do that?" They shot round as quickly as possible! Three days later our son was born, so it was very special really. My Christian faith is the same age as our son.

We were here for five years, and the grounding we got from Brian and Rosemary – from a biblical level, very straight-down-the-road Christianity, lovely home groups, the wonderful atmosphere there, the Christian fellowship, reading some good Christian books – it was a very rounded experience. There was good mentoring as well after we became Christians. And at the same time, they were almost like proxy grandparents to our son. It was a wonderful mixture of practical, hands-on help and spirituality.

Barry: Whenever they came to England we would see them. Quite extraordinarily, they moved to Exeter very shortly after us. Then they moved down to Exmouth and we visited quite regularly, so we kept in constant touch. Once or twice Brian came over to preach at our fellowship here in Crediton.

Denise: We always kept in touch when we were separated by distance. Of course, they were out in Sharjah, so there was less contact then, but there were letters and phone calls to touch base. We still have very good conversations, even just on the phone. We touch base with Giles from time to time as well, because of course we knew Giles when he was growing up. He would come back in school holidays to stay with his parents.

Barry: Brian's a very strong man for the gospel, and very good at preaching it. He is always appreciated wherever he goes. He's a fine man.

Barry and Denise run Hillbrow Residential Care Home in Crediton.

Dennis and Shelagh King

Dennis and Sheelagh King met the Bradleys during a service at St Andrew's Church in Cullompton, and were immediately keen for Brian and Rosemary to help with their Prison Fellowship work. They were involved in a long-term ministry at the local category B prison for men who were on remand and awaiting trial.

Dennis: I sat next to Rosemary, and after the service I asked her if she would be interested in prison work. She said, "I'll have to ask my husband." Afterwards, there was a gathering in the hall. We met Brian and explained to him what we did.

Sheelagh: We'd moved back here to Exeter in 1999, and I had wanted, for ten years, to go into prisons. I suppose I was called to it. I hadn't lived near a prison before, so it was a new opportunity. I started in the Education department, because at that time the Chaplain wasn't actually asking for outside help. Then they changed the Chaplain and the new one sent a message out to churches in Exeter, saying "Please come and help me!" So I went to help just after 2000.

Every Wednesday we met at what they called the Chaplain's Hour for about two hours. At that point there were two or three chaplains leading it. My husband was working at the time, so I went in with some other people who were interested, and we basically sat with the prisoners and followed whatever the lead chaplain wanted us to do. Later on, we took over running the afternoon sessions. I had no keys to the cells, but I had keys to get myself in and out of prison at that time. I did about thirteen-and-a-half years, and Dennis did 11 years.

Dennis: The men came for all sorts of reasons: to get out of their cells; to get tea and biscuits. A lot of them had serious issues they wanted to talk about. Some were Christians, and some we saw really go on in their faith. They were up and down, much like the rest of us! Brian, among others, would pray with them, and sometimes the Holy Spirit really touched them. We ran about seven Alphas in all. We had people come in to play the music, and different people gave talks. Brian is a really enthusiastic guy for sharing, and that sort of milieu really suited him. He used to get stuck in!

Sheelagh: Brian loved speaking particularly with one or two who really wanted to discuss things. When we did Alpha courses, he helped give one of the talks. He was always wanting to point men to Jesus. He had an infectious enthusiasm for the gospel and the men respected him.

Sometimes we had about sixteen prisoners. These were men who wanted to come. It was completely voluntary. One or two were serious about God, as much as they could be. We went in on Sundays once a month for the basic service they did, and Rosemary came in for that.

We have sat with murderers, obviously, and equally we've sat with people who had been drunk and disorderly. The atmosphere in the chapel was holy, and on the whole there was respect. It was a good place where people could grow in the Lord. It was God; it must have been. Even if they'd only come for tea and biscuits they were very respectful. They'd say, "Well it's not for me, but I enjoyed the tea!" That was a good time. It was about sowing seeds. We definitely had one or two prisoners, perhaps more than that, who stood for the Lord after prison. You could see them moving on towards Jesus.

Dennis
The attitude was not, on our part, "We must hit them over the head with the gospel." It was more, "Here's what we believe, but what would you like to talk about?" It was a sort of balancing act. Often, things would come up about the supernatural: tarot cards, stars and all that stuff. We'd sit around, and Brian was part of this. We'd say, "Let's see what the Bible says." Often, they would tell us how it had damaged them, rather than us telling them. We prayed for them, and sometimes they prayed for us!

Sheelagh: The Prison Fellowship met as a group once a month, and Brian and Rosemary were very good attendees. We shared news about what we had experienced in the prison, and built each other up.

Exeter Prison Fellowship took part each year in the international Angel Tree project, which arranges giving presents to the children of prisoners. One of our group used to buy presents suitable for the age of the child, and then we would have one or two sessions wrapping them up; eighty to a hundred presents in total. Brian was not very good at parcels, so Rosemary used to help him, but he was very keen.

The giving of these presents was very effective in helping the relationship of the prisoner and his family. The man was able to write a little note to his child, which was fixed to the present. As far as the child was concerned, the present came from Dad. We prayed over the presents and posted them, and sent the men a card to tell them what we had given their children.

Brian and Rosemary joined in with eager enthusiasm. They told their church in Littleham stories of what was happening in the prison, and encouraged them to give money for the presents. They were very successful at that and had a great heart for Angel Tree.

AUTHOR'S NOTE

This account is based partly on my own memory of the events that have taken place in my life to date. However, having suffered a mini stroke followed by a lengthy emergency operation on my carotid artery, my memory has been severely affected and my recollection of some of the finer details has diminished.

I thank God for the detailed records I kept during my time in ministry, which helped immensely in refreshing my memory of events. I have relied heavily on copies of the many 'obligatory' monthly reports I had to post on to headquarters in London from my three or four years serving with The Missions to Seamen Society in Ceylon (Sri Lanka), and have made use of supporting information from other reliable sources.

I have also made use of much information contained in my files concerning my work with the International Continental Church Society (ICS) in Amsterdam, as well as in Lyon and Grenoble, France.

It was fascinating to read back through these reports many years after I retired and to recall all that God had done during this time. Without them, I would have struggled to put together this testimony of his goodness.